Dear Mr. Su

Happy reading

With regards

Raju Menon.

23.09.2022

The VIEW from MY PERCH

The VIEW from MY PERCH

A 360-DEGREE VIEW
OF AN UNCHARTED LIFE

RAJU MENON

HarperCollins *Publishers* India

First published in India by HarperCollins *Publishers* 2022
4th Floor, Tower A, Building No. 10, Phase II, DLF Cyber City,
Gurugram, Haryana – 122002
www.harpercollins.co.in

2 4 6 8 10 9 7 5 3 1

P-ISBN: 978-93-5489-727-6
E-ISBN: 978-93-5489-728-3

The views and opinions expressed in this book are the author's own.
The facts are as reported by him, and the publishers
are not in any way liable for the same.

Raju Menon asserts the moral right
to be identified as the author of this work.

Cover design: Haitenlo Semy
Front cover photo: Firoze Edassery

Typeset in 12/16 Adobe Garamond Pro at
Manipal Technologies Limited, Manipal

Printed and bound at
Thomson Press (India) Ltd

I am what I am because of my family.

Contents

Life Stacked—In Random

Rajeev Chandrasekhar
राजीव चंद्रशेखर

सत्यमेव जयते

Minister of State for Skill Development &
Entrepreneurship and
Electronics & Information Technology
Government of India
कौशल विकास और उद्यमशीलता एवं
इलेक्ट्रॉनिकी और सूचना प्रौद्योगिकी राज्य मंत्री
भारत सरकार

Foreword

I HAVE READ WITH GREAT interest this book about Mr. Raju Menon. While it is of a biographical nature, it is also aimed at various demographic segments like youth, women, young entrepreneurs and professionals, hoping that it will inspire them to fulfil the wishes of Honourable Prime Minister Narendra Modi ji of an Atmanirbhar Bharat.

Towards this end, as a respected business leader who, even while living in a foreign land running businesses in multiple geographies, is contributing to driving that paradigm change foreseeing India as a vibrant, global force—not only business, but in several dynamic spheres, including as a spearhead of soft skills, culture and development. I am delighted to do the Foreword for this book about his life and times.

I sincerely hope that this story of the rise of a patriotic Indian from a small-town Kerala village to the pinnacle of achievements in one of the world's most competitive markets is read, assimilated and its invaluable lessons put into good practice by the variegated target audience of the book, especially the youth.

I wish Raju Menon more success, the scaling of greater heights and the very best for wide readership, recognition and accolades for this book around the world.

Jai Hind.

Rajeev Chandrasekhar

New Delhi
29 November 2021

Shram Shakti Bhawan, New Delhi - 110001, Phone : +91-11-23465816, Fax : +91-11-23465829
E-mail : mos-msde@gov.in
Electronics Niketan, CGO Complex, Lodhi Road, New Delhi - 110003, Phone : +91-11-24368757
Fax : +91-11-24360958, E-mail : mos-eit@gov.in

II Vice Chairman
ABU DHABI CHAMBER OF COMMERCE & INDUSTRY
غرفة تجارة وصناعة أبو ظبي

YUSUFF ALI. M.A.
Chairman & Managing Director

Head Office: Y Tower, Al Mamoura Street,
P.O. Box: 4048, Abu Dhabi, UAE
Tel: Direct: +971 2 6410786, Office: +971 2 4140870
Fax: +971 2 6421716, E-mail: yusuffma@ae.lulumea.com
www.lulugroupinternational.com

Message 1

TODAY WE ARE LIVING in a fast-paced life of fierce competition, where the task of proving oneself time and again has become the way of life. In order to survive and prove themselves, most of the people become players and sacrifice their dreams and ideals. However, very few refuse to remain just players and choose to be game-changers. Such people not only bring about a change in their lives but also become an inspiration to others to travel the unknown path and to fulfil their dreams.

One such game-changer is Raju Menon, an established Chartered Accountant in the UAE who was born and raised in a humble family in rural Kerala. His autobiography, *The View from my Perch*, is one such story in which he fondly remembers his mother, from whom he has absorbed the values of hard work, grit, ability and the perseverance to dream big and to fulfil them.

It is with sheer brilliance, hard work, ambition and ethics that today Raju heads one of the leading Audit and Business Consultancy firms in the Middle East.

The View from my Perch offers an insight into the struggles, challenges and triumphs of a common man set to achieve an uncommon goal. It is indeed a story of determination, perseverance and inspiration. It is a humble attempt by the author to share his story and encourage the readers to hold on to their dreams as he elucidates through his own life story that nothing is impossible to achieve with hard work, upright principles and the right attitude. I am sure this book will give its readers the much-needed confidence to soar high in life.

Yusuff Ali M.A.
04.01.2022

aarin
INSPIRED CAPITAL

Message 2

Rᴀᴊᴜ ᴍᴇɴᴏɴ'ꜱ ʟɪꜰᴇ-ꜱᴛᴏʀʏ ɪꜱ an inspiration to all those who seek a better life and dream big in their area of work. From the time he set out from India to build a new Life in Dubai, Raju dreamt big, kept his focus on his dream and built up a great successful professional practice that is a Global Star today. It was a life of trials and tribulations, of success and failures, of great joy and sorrow, but the dream endured! A must read for all who dream big.

T.V.Mohandas Pai,
Chairman,
Aarin Capital Partners.

26 January 2022

Aarin Capital Partners
Office No. 01, 5th Floor, '1 Sobha', 50, St. Marks Road, Bangalore 560001 Karnataka, INDIA
T 91 80 6847 4100

CHAPTER ONE

A Genesis

Perched atop the 15th floor of a gleaming steel-and-chrome tower overlooking the gently rippling waves of the Dubai Creek, I gaze at the view before me. The waters of the creek meander, drawn by the vision, ambition and foresight of Dubai, from their source miles away, and transform into the Dubai Canal as they snake past Business Bay through what was once a dusty piece of desert. They flow out into the Arabian Sea, spawning new ecosystems as varied as businesses. I cannot but wonder about the surreal dissimilitude between various phases of my life— its beginnings, thousands of miles away in a surrounding that is a complete antithesis of the vantage point from which I now look at the lofty towers and well laid out cityscape bustling with endless energy and an undying entrepreneurial zeal, where over decades dreams have been made and realized by people from all over the world, especially that narrow strip of land from where I hail—Kerala, India.

I remember how, for compiling my experiences, thoughts and vision into this compendium of life, I would spend time alone in an office meeting room, aptly named Meydan, usually a crucible of ideas, passions and discussions, but then often, as I collated my thoughts, a haven for ferreting into the past to dig out nuggets buried in the deep recesses of my mind.

The vast contrast between what I extract from personal history—my beginnings in the green, pristine villages of Kerala, barely touched by the trappings of modernity and development—and what I see from where I am sitting, with the iconic, world-renowned Burj Khalifa piercing the clouds like a dazzling diamond sword, tells me that I have been very lucky. Of late, I have become convinced that the life I have built (in this wonder of a country) is but a form of God's blessings, his reward to me and the next generation for the benevolence, magnanimity and kindness of my parents.

CHAPTER TWO

The Journey

I LOVE CARS.

But where I grew up, there were hardly any.

My recent acquisition—I can't believe a quadrennium has flown by since—a jet black Rolls Royce Ghost, the epitome of automotive luxury and engineering, while it slithers down the superb roads and highways of the UAE, would find it very tough to negotiate the narrow village roads and byways of my village in Kerala.

Oftentimes, while at the wheels of this iconic marque, I am driven back in time to the early days of my journey.

For someone who hails from a village where a lone decrepit bus, plying once in the morning as a mode of transportation for leaving the village caught in a time warp and escaping into greener pastures and in the evening, reversing the process to safely deposit one into the secure and warm confines of home, away from the buzz of the towns, the journey has at once both been smooth and bumpy, staid and exciting.

Mine was quite a simple beginning. It was a very laid back, uncomplicated and rustic background, where walking to the village school, studying a little and frolicking a lot were more the norm than any great ambitious plans for a starry future.

The way back from school would be fun, with naughty experiments and expeditions often diverting us from the straightforward, easy way home. We would take longer routes that would help us motley bunch of friends to engage in endeavours like pelting stones at ripe old mangoes dangling from the sprawling orchards of neighbours, squirming our way into their compounds stealthily, smuggling them out and gathering below the large banyan tree at the village temple to share the spoils.

With time, walks to school morphed into bus rides to college, then into an occasional pillion ride on friends' scooters and eventually into riding to work on my own bike.

But while undertaking those rickety rides on bumpy, pot-holed roads, never did it cross my mind that I would, one day, be driving around in a bespoke Rolls Royce in one of the most happening cities in the world, on the crossroads between the East and West.

CHAPTER THREE

The Adobe Abode

SOMETIMES LIFE'S IRONIES CAN be quite interesting. Eerie, even.

When on a quiet morning, I slip into the office meeting room Meydan and sit down to gather my thoughts about the days of yore, it is as if from the meeting room a straight line of vision helps me connect the dots of the past.

It is as if I can, through the chrome vista windows, look past the mushrooming monuments, sparkling skyscrapers, azure Arabian Sea and turquoise horizon, as if I was peering through a kaleidoscope replaying thoughts, images and visions of the past.

A past which began at the other end of that straight line of vision from Dubai, in a tiny hamlet called Edavilangu near Kodungallur, Kerala.

The early memories are scant, and they revolve mostly around the family.

The background was humble, the abode quite simple, hewn from adobe and held together with a rushed mixture of sand and cement, with a fencing of wiry shrubs that served more to demarcate than to protect.

It was in a way a little cruelly ironic and reflective of the reality that Achan—that is how I would respectfully address my father, a construction work supervisor, in our vernacular language, Malayalam—could not afford a sturdier fabrication of metal buttressing but had to make do with a simple earthen mould of a house with palm leaves for a roof, not out of any intellectual environmental concern, but because of our tough financial situation.

But as if to make up for that, he was a tower of strength for us in his own quiet way, one who did all the heavy lifting, working for long periods away from home to ensure that the fire kept burning in the family kitchen, that there was always food on the table and that the bills were paid on time.

Amma was in all ways the right partner to him. She was petite but even with her diminutive frame, she was a woman of superlative strength, both in toughness of character and physical prowess.

And they were attributes that stood her in good stead in her profession of midwifery, which demanded a lot of strength and grace under pressure, stamina to endure long and painful procedures, and the will to make every endeavour a success.

PART I

Continuum

CHAPTER FOUR

Off the Starting Block

As I sit down to pen a compendium of memories, thoughts, experiences and meanderings till date and how they have formed me and shaped my vision for tomorrow, I start with my earliest memories.

After a few days, that search for the first recollections ends and images come into sharp focus, invariably starting with mental pictures of my birthplace.

When I was born, on 23 March 1963 in Edavilangu village near Kodungallur town in Thrissur district of Kerala, India, my father, Unniparambath Kanichukulath Madhava Menon, was 34 years old and my mother, Ettuveettil Govinda Menon Suseela, was 28.

They named me Ettuveettil Madhava Menon Rajagopalan.

According to Hindu belief, Rajagopal is another name of Lord Krishna, and its Sanskrit origin is a combination of '*raja*' meaning 'king' and '*gopala*' meaning 'cowherd', both of which come together to mean 'king of cowherds', strongly alluding to his role as a leader.

I am not sure if at that point my parents had any clairvoyant vision about my future. It's most likely they didn't, but eventually I became the leader of a large team of very smart people and thankfully I continue to be so.

Most people would call me Raju, a shorter and dearer version of Rajagopalan.

My sister Indira, born in 1956, and brother Unnikrishnan, just three years elder to me, made up my immediate family then. My youngest sister Sathi Devi would complete it with her arrival in 1971.

With Achan being about 200 kilometres away in Coimbatore, a city in the neighbouring state of Tamil Nadu, for long periods, working at construction sites and fending for the family, I was always with Amma. I witnessed her extraordinary hard work, willingness to help people and empathy, and it was only natural that Amma became my role model.

While Achan was away, Amma was our provider, guardian, mentor, guide and teacher, all rolled into one.

There were two more people who, though not part of our nuclear family of six, were considered as such and were an intricate, indelible and intrinsic part of our household.

My Ammumma, Achan's mother's younger sister, Kalyaniyamma, was our guardian, and most of our childhood was spent with her.

While our parents were away for long periods, Ammumma always remained at home, taking care of us.

Yet another person who was an enduring part of the household and the growing up years was Anandam Chechi ('Chechi' means elder sister in Malayalam), my mother's first cousin, also born in Kodungallur near my native village and now 74 and living in my Kozhikode residence since 2009.

Chechi, who is unmarried, was not only with us through our childhood but still continues to spend long spells of time with us.

I particularly remember her taking me along to enrol me in school as Achan and Amma could not get back home due to work commitments and devotion.

To admit me to school earlier than the required joining age, she quietly changed my date of birth from 23 March 1963 to 28 July 1962.

In the absence of Achan and Amma, it fell upon Anandam Chechi to be our father, mother, guardian, chaperone and chef, all rolled into one—and she fulfilled all roles with utmost care.

Chechi was always part of the family, taking care of us when we were children. Even now, when we are back in Kozhikode on holiday, she is the one who lovingly serves us hot meals, still substituting for Amma.

If Ammumma and Anandam Chechi formed our support system during childhood, another ineffaceable, kind person cared for us siblings during our teenage years.

Anandam Chechi's younger sister, Ambikadevi Chechi from Kodungallur, was with us for many years until she got married. However, not long after, her husband sadly left her and their two daughters.

They had nothing to fall back on, and Amma's kindness shone through. She brought them to our home and educated the kids. One became a teacher in an aided school in Cheekilode after completing her Bachelor of Education, and the other earned a Bachelor of Commerce qualification.

Later, after I had moved to Dubai and started earning well enough, I did what was necessary for them to secure their lives.

Ambika Chechi, now 67, is settled in Cheekilode, Kozhikode.

We were very lucky that there was always somebody to guard us and care for us, someone always willing to help out with the many things that needed to be taken care of at home.

Our house in Edavilangu was the humblest of abodes, made of adobe, bricks made of laterite rock, with two small bedrooms, a hall and a kitchen, and with a thatched roof made out of palm leaves. Though very basic, it had an idyllic setting, built right in the middle of a spacious, luscious, verdant compound with two ponds in which I used to splash around with cousins and friends.

Among my vast army of cousins, I was very close to my second cousin K. Vishwanatha Menon, now around 66 years old, who married my elder sister. He is now a retired honorary Captain and has lived his entire post-service life in Kodungallur.

Even though my sister died in 1979, Vishwanatha Chettan and I still maintain a very good relationship. He is extremely helpful and caring by nature, and if I or any of his friends or relatives need a reliable hand to get something done, he is the go-to man. We keep in touch through frequent visits and phone calls.

As with a lot of Tharavads (Malayalam for ancestral homes), in our house, too, a corner in the thick shrubby area near the house was demarcated as a sacred area of sorts, and there the trees and bush were allowed to grow wild.

Although a lot of the houses would have a small shrine dedicated to snake worship in such a sacred and venerated corner, we did not have one, although we would religiously light a mud lamp, and offerings of milk, rice, flowers and plantains were proffered to invoke the serpent god's blessings on special occasions associated with the deity. We were not a particularly religious family.

Maybe quite the opposite.

Achan was a soft-spoken man, quite an introvert. He was formally educated only up to sixth class, but even while he was working as a construction worker and later as a supervisor overseeing iron rebar work in building projects, he was a bookworm. He was a voracious reader, and books were his constant companions. He had only a handful of friends throughout his life.

From those hazy early years, I remember clearly that he was a heavy smoker, puffing *beedis* frequently (they are cheaper, smaller, thinner versions of cigarettes, made of *tendu* leaves with a filling of tobacco flakes wrapped around and then tied up with a string). This was a habit that he gave up very late in life, when he was around 50. He was almost a teetotaller; I saw him have alcohol very rarely. Achan was very frugal in all ways, spending nothing on himself and entrusting all his earnings to Amma when he came home for off-season breaks from work—twice or thrice a year— during which he would be confined to his room, devouring every book that he could find from the nearby libraries.

He would lap up the biographies of Gandhiji and Nehru and read books on Kerala's Communist leaders, for whom he had special affection, even though his reclusive nature meant that he had no involvement in active politics.

He was particularly interested in Kerala and Indian history and was impressed by the social changes the Communists had brought about in Kerala during the Independence struggle and thereon. This helped shape his strong political convictions and probably explained why there was no insistence by Achan on religious observances by the family.

Achan considered Amma his anchor. She was everything for him.

In her he saw and appreciated a very strong, independent lady who would not only take care of the children and household chores while he was away but also work as hard as or harder than himself to bring in another much-needed income to the household.

If anyone needed proof for the adage opposites attract, my parents' relationship would be the ideal testament.

For Amma was the perfect contrast to Achan.

If Achan was an introvert, Amma was the total opposite. Achan could be quite sceptical at times, but Amma was always positive.

Achan entrusted all he had to Amma. She would generously help as many people as she could.

Amma was well known for her kindness and good-naturedness; at any given time, there would be a long list of people who had requested her for support.

But with a smile, she would give away whatever she had and, often, more.

If Achan often took long breaks between work, Amma worked non-stop for 24 hours, defying the laws of science to complete seemingly impossible assignments—such as taking tuitions, doing midwifery tasks, managing the home, taking care of us children—a vast array of tasks in 24 hours, all 365 days of the year.

Even with their almost irreconcilably contrasting demeanours and attitudes, Achan and Amma created a warm nest for all of us, with just enough to go by but nevertheless content with what we had, not too many big aspirations putting pressure on any of us.

And that was something I wanted to replicate when I grew up, even though my life at that point was at a blissfully blithe stage—there was no focus, no clear plans on how to do it or anything for that matter, but just a liking for contentment and a desire to have a well-knit, happy family.

Even if while growing up with them I could not correctly gauge the impact my family members would have on my life, I would later realize the defining way in which each shaped me, in various ways and scales.

But most importantly Amma, with her overflowing kindness, sheer hard work, dedication and commitment to the tasks at hand, pleasant nature and brilliant communication skills.

For her, every venture she undertook had to be a 100 per cent success. There could be no other ending. Any other result would have been disastrous.

Perhaps that is how and when I first learnt that I need to get things right from the start, all the time.

CHAPTER FIVE

The First Centripetal Moves Begin

SOME OF THE EARLIEST scenes that come to mind, even if hazy, are my walks, almost a kilometre long, to Edavillangu Government High School, Kodungallur, where I was a student from 1967 until I completed my fourth class in 1971. As with most government-run schools of the time, the medium of education was Malayalam, and this would continue till I finished schooling.

With both Achan and Amma being from Kodungallur, we had a lot of cousins of various ages living close by, with whom I grew up. Though the extended family was very large—around 70–80 nuclear families—my siblings and I were very close to around 20 cousins.

In the mist of memory, I clearly remember one friend, Fazulu Huq.

He was my companion on our strolls to school, my partner as we frolicked in the ponds around the house and Amma's student as she tutored him.

In 1971, after I turned eight, we had to move from Edavilangu in Thrissur district to an unfamiliar Kadungalloor in Valavannoor Panchayat, Malappuram.

The only familiarity I had with the new home was the close phonetic similarity with the old. There ended any connection.

The move was only over a 150-kilometre shift in terms of geographical distance. But in supplanting oneself from a familiar environment, with all its support systems, to a completely alien one, it was a sea change, literally and littorally, as we moved away from a coastal village by the Arabian Sea and into the hinterland, climbing higher in altitude, too, as we settled into our new turf.

The move was necessitated as Amma, who was working as a midwife with a government hospital, was given a transfer.

In the seventies, Kerala, especially northern Kerala, had a distinct lack of quality healthcare facilities and trained professionals, a deficiency that subsequent governments addressed and corrected to make the state a model in providing world-renowned standards not only in hospital and medical infrastructure, but also education and other key human development indices.

Various United Nations' bodies have acknowledged the progress made; it is now referred to as the Kerala model of development.

One of the key areas in which northern Kerala lagged behind at the time was pregnancy and childbirth care, and midwives played a very crucial role in offering care and support during the various stages of pregnancy to women. Their role was especially critical when it came to the later stages of pregnancy—labour, delivery and post-birth.

Amma, being an extrovert and a skilled communicator, adapted quickly to the ambience and sensibilities of the people of Kadungalloor, quietly and quickly earning their respect and trust for her diligence, dedication and sincerity that always put the people and their comfort and well-being ahead of everything else, even at the cost of personal sacrifices.

I was in quiet awe of the strength, resilience and laser-sharp focus Amma displayed as she handled the straightforward cases and the complicated ones with the same ease, calm and confidence.

I vowed to myself then that no matter what challenges life threw at me, I would remain unfazed and composed like Amma. I believe I have mostly been able to abide by that promise.

Meanwhile, I was settling well into the life at Kadungalloor.

We were staying at a small, cosy annex of the Health Centre there, surrounded by greenery.

My school, Aided Upper Primary School, funded by the government was just over six kilometres away in Kozhakkottoor, Aricode, where I studied from Class 5 to Class 7 between 1971 and 1974. The journey to school involved a bit of a walk along the beautiful, tree-lined village roads and a short bus ride. My close friend Ibrahim, who stayed nearby, was my constant companion on the way to school and back. We would mostly have fun, unencumbered by any large inspiration or ambition.

My other close friend, Abdul Rahman, was very interested in politics and had good awareness of the latest happenings. Regular discussions with him on this subject aroused an interest in me as well. It was a childhood of pure, innocent bliss.

As they say, change is the only constant. And in my life, it was an ever-recurring constant.

Once again, just as I was getting used to the trips to the school, neighbours and friends, a change was warranted as our school taught students up to upper primary only. For high school, which is defined as classes 8–10 in Kerala's educational norms, I had to move to the nearest available option—Government Higher Secondary School, Kuzhimanna, Kizhissery, Malappuram. A five-kilometre bus ride away.

This was in June 1974.

Life at this new school, too, was short-lived. After completing just one year there, after I had finished my eighth class, it was time for the next dash.

When I look back, I think that a lot of the flexibility, perseverance and nimbleness that I possess now are a result of the frequent changes in my life and my responses to shield myself from the impacts of the disruptions and the unsettled state of mind that probably followed such altered ecosystems.

I do not think I experienced any direct impact then; maybe I was too young to realize even if there was one, but I guess there was a deep, subliminal footprint.

Once more, we had to change course anew as Amma was transferred again to another government health centre.

And as was the wont with government jobs, just as Achan, Amma and all of us were getting used to a new life, we had to move on and start afresh.

This time, we moved to a place just 50 kilometres from the coast and slightly lower in altitude. Nevertheless, it was a very similar landscape, with dense woods and a rustic backdrop.

Cheekilode, Kozhikode, was to be the new home. Yet another beginning.

My new school: Kolathur Government Higher Secondary School, now known as Swami Guruvarananda Memorial Government Higher Secondary School, Kolathur, Kozhikode. New friends: Raveendran, Ramachandran, Rajeevan, Prabhakaran. Additionally, I had new neighbours, new locales along a three-kilometre walk to school and new playgrounds.

Life in the new school began with the academic year of 1975.

The school calendar mostly begins on the first of June when usually the monsoon rains, if on time, accompany the flow of students to schools for a drenched beginning. June started in the same fashion that year, too.

But just three weeks later, on 25 June 1975, the dreaded Emergency was declared.

Too young to understand its political and societal ramifications, all I remember of that period is the enhanced police patrolling.

Due to the strict censorship, most people in Kerala were oblivious to what was happening in the northern states of India, where some draconian measures were implemented to curb the freedom of citizens.

This gave rise to a lot of anger against the government. There was tumult all around, and the then all-powerful Prime Minister Indira Gandhi was defeated in the first elections held during that infamous period of Indian history.

Surprisingly, with Kerala not having been impacted much and most people believing that the strict measures had done good for the state—even though there were a few lock-up torture issues that came to light after the Emergency—Congress-led fronts were very successful in the 1977 elections, both for the Parliament and Assembly.

In the Kerala Legislative Assembly elections held on 19 March 1977, to elect members to the fifth Niyamasabha, the United Front, led by the Indian National Congress and the Communist Party of India (CPI), won the majority of seats and stayed on in power, with K. Karunakaran as the Chief Minister.

Whereas in the Indian Parliamentary elections, for the first time, the Congress-led Front won all 20 seats in Kerala, validating the notion that Keralites were not adversely impacted and that they liked the disciplinary measures imposed in the state.

Today, Swami Guruvarananda Memorial GHSS, Kolathur, Kozhikode, looks spiffy. With smart architecture, sturdy construction, bright paint and well-equipped labs, the government-run schools in the state give private schools a run for their money.

But in our days, they painted a completely different, ramshackle picture.

When my classmates, batchmates and I joined, there were no proper classrooms.

As we were the first batch in school, after completing the first three classes of the day, then referred to as periods, for the next two we would be asked, with official permission from the school authorities, to go out to nearby houses and collect coconut palm leaves woven by the families and bring them back to school.

Labourers would then stack them over the roof woodwork, which would provide shelter from sun and rain, although when it rained heavily, most of the rainwater would still seep through and drench us.

Some of the leaves would be used as separators between classrooms, but most of the happenings in the neighbouring classes would be visible to students on both sides of the divide.

This was a regular phenomenon for several years.

Being a new, underfunded school then, there was always a shortage of staff.

Due to that, the same teacher would teach us English, Mathematics and Science, which meant that we had just one instructor for the three periods in a day.

Luckily for us, he did not know Hindi and did not teach us that subject.

Our school would have set a world record of sorts had that teacher known a bit of Hindi, for he would have been a rare teacher on Planet Earth instructing students in four major subjects that were critical to their future.

But at least one thing was sure. This schooling could only last for a maximum of two years as, according to the prevalent education system in Kerala at the time, one's school life would be over after Class 10, and it would be a coming of age of sorts as students would then necessarily have to go to college for further education.

But in my case, there would be a change even to that.

More on that twist later.

So, two years of none-too-focused studies, collecting and weaving palm leaves, teenage fun and games and a bit of music and films meant that almost in parallel with the ending of the Emergency in March 1977, I was getting close to the end of my school days and, quite like the India that emerged after the clampdown, did not know what was in store for me.

CHAPTER SIX

A Stinging Parallel Education

IT WAS CRUNCH TIME.

After a life of freewheeling nonchalance, not caring too much about the present or future and just having fun and gliding along from class to class, my Secondary School Leaving Certificate examination (SSLC; Class 10) results were out.

As expected, they were disappointing. I had barely scraped through, ending up with low marks in almost every subject.

And it meant that I could not, unlike most of my classmates, get into what should have been the next natural choice—an entry into a pre-degree course (combination of Class 11 and Class 12) in an established college affiliated to an approved university, which would also allow me to pick what my future course of study and career would be.

For most Indian students, according to the educational systems prevalent then, this phase was a turning point in their life and career, where they moved from the strict confines and rules of school life to a rather open and liberal college atmosphere. Here, one could participate in a bit of student politics, indulge in more robust extra-curricular activities and, in most cases, mix with students of the opposite gender.

That is also when the best and brightest in school would naturally gravitate to the prime options—the First Group (Physics, Chemistry, Maths, English, Indian/Foreign Language, e.g. Hindi/Malayalam/French) for those who preferred Engineering and allied streams, Second Group (Physics, Chemistry, Biology, English, Indian/Foreign Language) for those interested in Medicine and related fields such as Dentistry, Nursing, Pharmacy, Agriculture, etc., Third Group (Economics, Indian History, World History, English, General Education, Indian/Foreign Language) aimed at those keen on Economics and Humanities and Fourth Group (Accountancy, Commerce, Commercial Correspondence, Commercial Geography, General Education, English, Indian/Foreign Language) for professions such as Chartered Accountancy and related careers.

But I was stuck in a morass. While most of my friends, by virtue of the good marks obtained in their SSLC, had entered the vibrant, exciting environs of college campuses, I had to settle for the only available option—parallel college, which was the refuge of those who formed the last group of students, those with the least marks, to continue their education.

These were no fancy colleges with elegant buildings, great reputations, huge libraries, qualified teachers, indulgent extra-curricular activities, fancy campuses and good canteens; they were often the very basic, quickly constructed sheds with newly qualified graduates making up the teaching staff.

One such college was Chelannur Arts College, a very basic parallel college in Chelannur, Kozhikode, about six kilometres away from my residence then at Cheekilode Health Centre.

Covering the distance partly on foot and partly on a bicycle with friends, I completed the two years of pre-degree education, vowing to myself that I would never again be content with mediocrity and that I would get into a regular college after these two difficult years, during which my friends had left me behind and were enjoying superior-quality education.

For the first time in my life, the medium of teaching was English. However, with a lot of the students like me coming from Malayalam medium schools, the teachers would mostly converse in the mother tongue.

Often, like most of my companions, I too had to learn some of the content by heart without understanding the meaning, due to our lack of proficiency in the English language.

This, I realized, was a handicap that needed correction.

I was dejected. I was just 15 and felt utterly alone in my inferior educational surroundings while my schoolmates enjoyed their new-found freedom, picking up new communication skills and relishing the thrills of campus life. But then I decided to take on a challenge—I would leverage the opportunity I had and move on, never to be content with the ordinary.

Even today, I hold that character trait dear. I always try to excel.

After a month at the parallel college, as I was determined to outdo myself, I got entry into a nearby college, Sree Narayana Guru College, Chelannur, to study the Fourth Group.

Having already settled into the new atmosphere at the parallel college, paid the fees, made friends and established a good relationship with the teachers, I decided that to lose the fees and then pay it again to the new institute was not worth it. So I stayed back and decided to study my B.Com in Sree Narayana Guru College after two years.

Money was very hard to come by. There was very little to be wasted.

That stinging rejection that I suffered due to my lack of focus and hard work and my time at the parallel college had steeled my resolve.

I would never settle for the mundane again. Ever.

CHAPTER SEVEN

Re-joining the Mainstream

First Test of Resolve

FOR PROBABLY THE FIRST time in my life, stung hard by the necessity of having to make do with the worst option, I worked very hard.

For the first time, my focus on the task at hand was laser-sharp—I had to get enough marks to secure admission in a regular, reputed college.

The pre-degree exams were held during the scorching summer months of April and May.

In early June, along with the monsoon rains, which bring much-needed relief for Kerala, cooling the parched lands, feeding its rivers and streams and rejuvenating the withering vegetation, I felt relieved at tasting success. I had a score that would normally have got me entry into a degree course in commerce, this time in an educational institution of repute.

More importantly, I had passed the first test of resolve.

I realized then that if I set a goal and worked hard towards it, I could achieve it. I knew that it would be a modus operandi I would follow throughout my life.

I had not read any fancy management books about goal-setting; my reading was very limited then and even my language skills were mostly confined to Malayalam. At that time, there were not too many such books or magazines in Malayalam. My realization came because I had experienced it first-hand.

The college closest to Cheekilode was Sree Narayana Guru College, Chelannur, within Kozhikode and just five kilometres away by the usual means of transport—a short walk and then a bicycle ride with friends.

My close friends at college were P.K. Janardhanan, A.M. Vijayan and M. Dilipkumar, and we enjoyed every bit of the campus life.

So that was a turning point of sorts too. For the first time in my life, I would have to interact closely with a language other than Malayalam, a language that was the lingua franca of Kerala and India and a must-have if one was to achieve lofty ambitions.

Slowly but surely, in a more sophisticated college ambience, exposure to qualified and experienced teachers, structured studies of subjects that I was beginning to like and concentrate on and expansion of horizons, firm ideas and plans were taking shape, even if I did not yet have a clue as to what would happen or what my future would be.

But from a life of zero focus, there emerged the faint hints of a general direction.

So when I had finished three years of degree education, from 1979 to 1982, I was finally a graduate.

Friends at college who came from Kozhikode city were talking about the lucrative prospects after completing a very tough Chartered Accountancy (CA) course, and I was inspired.

As CA firms were based in metropolitan areas and I had only very limited knowledge of Kozhikode city and an even narrower friends circle there, I managed to approach only one firm there that had sizable practice during those days. And I was not given a chance.

Disappointed and thinking it was beyond me, I did not make any further attempts then. One door had been slammed shut.

My next options? I could get a job or I could go for further education. Unsure about which way to go, I tried out both options.

I was keen to get a job and start earning so that I could take care of the family.

By then I had also begun to dream of and aspire for a significantly better life and lifestyle and was also considering an M.Com degree, which would possibly lead me to a remunerative career.

During the four-month gap between finishing B.Com and starting M.Com, I applied for a job with a regional rural bank, South Malabar Gramin Bank, headquartered in Malappuram, with operations limited to just eight districts in Kerala.

Its main lines of business were financing ventures in agricultural and non-agricultural sectors and running other employment generation programmes through its 506 branches spread over these eight districts.

I passed the qualification test, but could not clear the personal interview.

One more door slammed shut with a bang. This was also a wake-up call and a slap on my face.

(Later on, in July 2013, with glee and amusement, I read that by amalgamating South Malabar Gramin Bank and a similar rural bank, North Malabar Gramin Bank, a new single entity branded Kerala Gramin Bank was created, with its head office in Malappuram. I thanked the management and my stars for rejecting my job application, wondering what would have happened had I got the role.)

Even now, my wife jokes that her lucky charm worked its magic on me, or I would still have been cycling between home and work at that bank.

Suddenly, from the three available options, two were eliminated, and the remaining one was hanging by a tiny thread.

As I was planning to become a CA, I had not applied to any college for pursuing an M.Com degree.

In a flash, it dawned on me that I would not get a registration for that professional course in the only firm I knew. I also realized, with alarm, that most colleges had stopped accepting applications for master's degree courses.

I was a wreck and ran helter-skelter, calling up friends and contacts to know which colleges were still accepting applications so that I could get into a reputed one at any cost. I did not want to slide back into the parallel college days. I found that there was just one college still open for admissions and that the closing date was that very day.

I rushed to submit my M.Com application at Government College Madappally at Vadakara, Kozhikode, barely met the deadline and handed over all the required forms and documents to the staff concerned at the counter, breathing a sigh of relief.

Having done the needful, I stepped out of the office, looked around the spacious, beautiful, lush pastoral campus, with posters of Che Guevera, Fidel Castro and other leftist icons adorning the walls.

Then I went to the canteen, got myself a cup of tea and thus began the wait.

It was a long, painful interval, during which I eagerly awaited a call for college admission.

I looked to the only open escape route to the future, hoping it would not be barricaded. And then the call came. A dramatic, impactful chapter of my life was to begin far away from home, in Kozhikode.

CHAPTER EIGHT

The Adobe Abode Turns Concrete

ACHAN AND AMMA WOULD start all over again.

And now, in my teenage years, as I was able to gather more memories, sponge up more experiences, collate variegated insights, store more thoughts and analyse them more deeply, I began to appreciate even more what parents and family meant to me.

In the new stage of life, Achan and Amma once again diligently continued their work and the onerous task of taking care of all of us.

The nature of Amma's job meant she bore the brunt of it all—being called at odd hours to help yet another woman in great pain, working long hours to ensure that all her efforts bore fruit, each endeavour bringing another bundle of joy into the world and filling the parents with happiness and thus also earning the enormous gratitude and well wishes of many.

Some cases would be normal and relatively easy to handle. Others would be complicated breech births or twin births or even the odd triplets. Fully aware that securing the futures of two lives—those of the mother and the baby—was her responsibility, Amma would spend all her focus and energy on the job at hand.

Often, a lot of physical and mental strength had to be drawn upon, and it was not rare to see her spend even up to 14 hours at a time helping a woman bring a newborn into the world, mothering them both through the incessant pain of new life.

It was not difficult to gauge, from the quiet pride and satisfaction with which Amma came home after each such case, that to be of service to humanity would be one of the things I would aspire to when my time came.

For Amma, by now, needing a safe haven after her peripatetic life of many years, a secure sanctuary to return to after long hours at work, was a necessity.

With Achan leading a roving life and Amma having lived in very humble adobe abodes and in health centre annexes for years, and with their kids growing up, they decided that it was time to build a concrete, albeit basic, house, both literally and figuratively, the raw earthen material to be replaced by durable cement and of course rebar, the iron rod, the moulding of which into usage in construction was Achan's area of specialization.

Achan had entrusted all his earnings to Amma, who in turn had added a bit of her own savings, but the pile of money needed for the new house—the cost of the land and the construction— would come from selling a large chunk of our ancestral land in Kodungallur, about 60 cents (0.6 acres, nearly 2,430 square metres) at about ₹11,000 (with US$1 = ₹9.46 in 1982, then worth US$1,162.80), per cent netting around ₹660,000, equivalent of US$69,767.00.

We were happy that we had got a decent amount for the land.

But that glee turned to disappointment as we learned that the land was immediately resold to another buyer for a huge profit.

There was talk among people that the buyer was from one of the Gulf countries and that a lot of money made there rather easily, comparing the work to the remuneration, was being ploughed back to buy land and luxury in Kerala.

I was very curious to know how that worked, and I gathered that several such people who became rich quickly were from Dubai.

A seed was sown. I wanted to go to Dubai too. To try my luck. There were no concrete plans yet, but subliminally, a new vista had opened up, a new option had been quietly created.

With the newly accumulated money, our first concrete house took shape, a small house in the middle of 40 cents of land with a lot of shady trees and thick shrubs around, and this time with the greater security of strong walls, a proper roof and iron grills to let in the light and facilitate cross-ventilation.

Such was our social and familial milieu at that time that even though all of us wanted to have an attached and covered car shed, we were overly worried about what relatives, neighbours and friends might think of our audacious wish to own a car at a time when even sustenance was hard.

So, fearful of probable rebuke and sly, pointed questions from our near and dear ones, that ambition was quietly dropped.

Little did we think, even in our wildest dreams, that one day our house would have several extensions, including a car garage, in which the latest cars would be parked. And thus, in 1982, our first dream home was built in Cheekilode, Kozhikode district, about 162 kilometres from our ancestral base of Kodungallur, Thrissur.

This was the first of my migratory settlements. Many were to follow.

CHAPTER NINE

Sojourn Number One

HAVING BEEN REJECTED BY the rural bank and gained admission at the very last minute to Government College Madappally at Vadakara, Kozhikode district, I started in earnest to complete the M.Com degree with good grades.

In more ways than one. My college was far away from the confines of home. A walk or a cycle ride would not take me there.

A bus ride from home in Cheekilode along the shortest route lined by a lush, verdant landscape would take me from around 60 metres above the sea level down a winding road to Kappad—known for its splendid beach—where it would join National Highway 66, and further along the coast via Koyilandy, Payyoli and Vadakara to reach the college, a distance of about 50 kilometres in under 90 minutes.

Kappad finds a mention in history and geography texts as the gateway to the Malabar Coast. On 8 July 1497, Vasco da Gama led a fleet of four ships with a crew of 170 men from Lisbon, sailing along the coast of Africa via Tenerife and Cape Verde Islands. After reaching the coast of present-day Sierra Leone, da Gama took a course south into the open ocean, crossing the Equator and seeking the South Atlantic westerlies that Bartolomeu Dias had discovered in 1487.

The fleet arrived in Kappad near Kozhikode (Calicut) in the Malabar Coast (present-day Kerala) on 20 May 1498.

A stone monument installed by the government commemorates the 'landing' by Vasco da Gama with the inscription, 'Vasco da Gama landed here, Kappakadavu, in the year 1498'.

Government College Madappally is situated on a green hillock, seven kilometres north of Vatakara, with the Arabian Ocean visible in the distant horizon to the west. The campus is rich with flourishing flora, having all the lushness and serenity of a rural retreat. The college was established in 1958 and had a six-decade-long glowing academic record thereafter. It was shifted to a new building in 1963, and more courses were introduced, marking the first major shift since its beginning. The college became the hub of higher education in northern Malabar and north Kerala in the 1960s. In 1968, the college was separated from the University of Kerala and affiliated to the University of Calicut.

While at the college between 1982 and 1984, I enjoyed the exciting campus atmosphere and made some good friends, like Sunil, Dinesan and Thomas, along with whom I had a great time, revelling in the present moment and planning for the future at the same time.

The reputed and experienced professors and lecturers who taught our class were very creative in their teaching methods and instilled in all of us a deep love and passion for the subjects.

This rekindled my dream to take up the challenging CA course; the pot of gold that it promised also lured me.

My move to the college also triggered my thought process and reinforced my faith in my ability to complete the course successfully.

Once in a while, after classes on weekends, I would take a bus trip from the college into the city. The route was the same up to Kappad, where the bus to Cheekilode would take a left from the junction while the one to the city would carry on along the coastal road and reach Kozhikode in about one and a half hours.

Over the two years of the M.Com course I familiarized myself with the layout of the city and the business environment and dynamics, made friends with people and when I graduated, I had enough marks and a strong network that could be tapped into if required.

But whenever I think of those days, I am invariably drawn to an absurdly hilarious episode. I cannot but recount this incident that terrorized my friends and me during our stay in Madappally, but now when we look back at it, evokes bouts of laughter.

My classmate Thomas and I were staying along with two bankers in a rented house. One night, while having a drunken celebration at the house, one of the bankers, in a wildly inebriated state, wanted to get some chicken and cook a dish.

Instead, we cooked up a mess.

While completely drunk, he happened to hear the cackle of a chicken from the neighbour's house and, with the illogical Dutch courage, he wanted to ensnare the bird and have it for dinner.

Some of us, less drunk, and hence more logical, objected furiously, knowing what the repercussions might be.

But the banker, in his state of wild intoxication, would have nothing to do with rationality.

So, convincing himself that the chicken was not from the neighbour's house but belonged to a household further away from us and therefore that there was no risk in stealing it, he went ahead, caught the chicken, brought it home and slaughtered it.

Just as we were about to cook a delicious meal, we heard the neighbour near our house, calling the chicken back to the coop.

We knew we were in trouble. We hid the mainour and a hush fell over the room.

But the suspicious neighbour, sensing that the bachelors in the rented house had something to do with the disappearance of the bird, refused to give up.

As the night progressed and the effect of the alcohol wore off and our hangover cleared, we came to know that the talk of the neighbourhood was the missing chicken and that some folks were pointing to us as the culprits.

The scene got worse, and soon a very angry crowd of people from the vicinity gathered near our house, accusing us, swearing at us and demanding that we own up to the crime and pay for it.

With that mob surrounding us and hurling the worst abuses, we were both humiliated and scared, knowing that any moment they could turn violent and harm us.

We pleaded innocence.

Our landlord came to know about the incident and promptly evicted us all from the house within a week's time.

Our nasty reputation had spread in that area, and it also made its way to our college, which was very close by. Everyone ridiculed and humiliated us for the chicken robbery. There was no way I could stay on in the college and the area. I was forced to take a long leave and I completed the remaining syllabus through self-study.

Even now, sometimes when I have a chicken dish, I break into a cackle at the memory.

CHAPTER **10**

An Uncharted Course

IN JULY 1984, WHEN the results of the M.Com exams were published, I had very good marks in all subjects—Accounting, Cost and Management Accounts, Economics, Taxation and Public Finance—obtaining a combined total that was considered a creditable score for a master's degree at the time. My favourite course was, obviously, Accounting, and I loved Economics.

But I was in a dilemma of sorts too. Should I get a job and take care of the family? Or should I pursue my passion and set a course for uncharted territory—CA had a fearsome reputation of being a very tough and challenging course with high standards—and spend many more years of uncertainty, the only attraction being the possibility of a very remunerative career at the end of years of struggle.

Often in my life I have been accused, by friends and family, of having an almost irrational approach to certain matters. One accusation, and a very crucial one at that, was regarding my quick decision-making and, once the decision was made, its even quicker implementation with strict milestones.

So it was one of those junctures, one of those confounding crossroads in life, where, bombarded with a slew of confusing thoughts, apprehensions and options, I had to look at the possible paths, choose the one I thought best as per the computations and then move quickly to my destination on a route from which there was no turning back.

So do I get a job or study to become a CA? Driven by passion or irrational exuberance? At that time, it was possibly both.

But as is my wont, and guilty as charged often by kith and kin, I took the very tough, bumpy road to my passion which had turned into an obsession by then.

Come what may, I was going to join the CA course, hoping that it would fetch me much better returns than a regular job would have, so that I would successfully be able to take care of my family.

Using the vast contact network I had developed by then, I was on the search for the best firm in Kozhikode, the one that would give me a tough grounding for the taxing curriculum.

The history of Chartered Accountancy in India begins as far back as in 1913, during the British rule, when it was stipulated under The Companies Act that several books were required to be maintained by a registered company.

To ensure the integrity and veracity of the registers, an auditor was required to maintain these books. The basic qualification to work as an auditor was a certificate from the local government.

In those days, there were two categories of auditors: the Unrestricted Certificate holder, who had the freedom to act as an auditor throughout the country, and the Restricted Certificate bearer, who could only act within the allotted province or conduct business in the language specified in the certificate.

Over the years, as businesses expanded and became more complex, the profession also evolved to handle the increasing intricacies.

In 1918, a diploma course named Government Diploma in Accounting (GDA) was started in Sydenham College of Commerce and Economics, Bombay. Candidates who wished to complete the diploma course were required to do an articleship for three years and had to pass the examination. The qualified candidates were rewarded with the Unrestricted Certificate, which was the precursor to the contemporary CA. In 1920, the issuance of Restricted Certificates also ended, thereby creating the first professional certification that was valid nationwide.

In 1927, an informal group of well-known and respected accounting professionals came together to form the Society of Auditors in Madras. It was formally registered as a Society in 1932 and was then the only body of accounting professionals that acted as a bridge between the profession and the government.

By 1930, after the Society was instituted in Madras, the Government of India decided to keep a record of the members practicing as auditors. The register was called the Register of Accountants and the professionals whose names were enlisted in the register were called Registered Accountants.

With the profession gaining more importance, in 1932, the Government decided to form an accountancy board to advise the Governor General in the Council of India on the finer points of accountancy and the required conduct along with qualification standards of the auditors. It was called the Indian Accountancy Board and it held its first examination in the year 1933.

The Institute of Chartered Accountants of India, ICAI, on their website describe that historic move: 'The Indian Accountancy Board set up in 1932 to regulate the accountancy profession and constituted after the Indian Companies' (Amendment) Act, 1930, came into force, had 16 members selected from all provinces—namely, Bombay, Bengal, Madras, United Province, Punjab, Central Province and Burma.'[1]

In the early years of the new accountancy board, GDAs were exempted from taking the test of auditors. But by 1943, GDA was completely abolished and the first qualifying examination for aspiring auditors was conducted by the Indian Accountancy Board.

With lingering fears and doubts that the accountancy profession was largely unregulated, causing much concern and confusion regarding the qualifications of auditors, after India's Independence, an expert committee was constituted in 1948 to look into the matter and make the necessary recommendations.

This was again a pivotal moment, which the ICAI extols as follows:

Few among us would be aware that it was the Board's Expert Committee appointed in 1948, which had examined the tentative scheme of an autonomous body for accountancy education under the chairmanship of Shri C. C. Desai, who

---

1   President's Message. The Institute of Chartered Accountants of India (ICAI). 1 July 2015. Available at https://www.icai. org/post.html?post_id=11779#:~:text=The%20Indian%20 Accountancy%20Board%20set,Punjab%2C%20Central%20 Province%20and%20Burma.

was then Secretary to the Ministry of Commerce, Govt. of India. The Committee had the privilege of drafting the Chartered Accountants Bill. Then it was this Committee that had decided to call the special Act as Chartered Accountants Act.[2]

The ICAI further goes on to say: 'It was again the Expert Committee that had officially brought about the much-desired parity among various practitioners of accountancy; it said that accountants in India would be called Chartered Accountants and no other designation would be used in India.'[3]

This expert committee recommended that a separate autonomous association of accountants should be formed to regulate the profession. The Government of India accepted the recommendation and passed the Chartered Accountants Act in 1949, even before India became a republic. Under the Act, ICAI was established on 1 July 1949 as a statutory body for regulating the profession of Chartered Accountancy in India.

So, after failing at my first attempt to join the respected, challenging and, at the end, a very remunerative course, I signed up with the ICAI and obtained an articleship in one of the city's most famous training grounds, U. Parasurama Iyer & Co., established in 1967 and situated right in the heart of the city, very close to Gandhi Park, Kozhikode.

The principal partner, CA M.V. Venugopal, was well known in the business circles of Kozhikode and Kerala, and a lot of

---

2   Ibid.

3   Ibid.

trainees under him have made their mark. I hoped I would make that grade too one day.

Though home was only around 45 minutes away by bus, due to the long hours at the firm and the taxing study schedule, I decided to stay in the city itself to focus on the rigours of work, which was a great practical learning exercise and also included voluminous theory.

With a strong network of friends and contacts by now, I joined a hostel called Central Technical College—CTC—Hostel, whose main occupants were students of varying courses.

It was a quick hop away from the workplace, just around one kilometre, which could be covered in five minutes. It was a great blessing to get a place there.

Though it was originally meant for CTC students, it was later opened to other students as well.

Quickly the number of CA students swelled and the CTC student numbers dwindled. In jest we rebranded the hostel as the CA Students' Training College Hostel.

In CTC, most of the CA students of our time passed the tough exams and qualified as members of the ICAI, except maybe three or four who unfortunately did not clear. All of us considered it to be a lucky hostel for CA students.

We had a great time together, being extremely close and supportive and helping each other not only in studies, but also for having a whale of a time while partying and celebrating.

M.J. Thankachan was the master of revelling. He would always store a pint of rum in his suitcase and frequently, once in a fortnight, he would take me in confidence to give him company.

We all put in about 12–14 hours of studies during our study leave period, which is usually arranged two to three months before the exams. To break the monotony and take a welcome break from intense studies, once in a month we would have a liquor party in high spirits and go out together to watch a movie.

Since all of us would be off articleship work at the CA firm to concentrate on studies, our gang of about 10 was together for most of the time. We would always go out for breakfast, lunch and dinner as a group to nearby restaurants during our study leave.

Breakfast would usually be at Potti's mess, which had a choice of vegetarian dishes such as *puttu* (steamed rice), lentils, *idlis* and crisp *dosas* and *vadas*.

For lunch and dinner, the favoured destination was Rainbow Restaurant.

All of us would be walking in a horizontal line stretched across the road, and passing motorists would honk at us and shout to express their displeasure. Very young and brash, we would hurl the abuses right back and have a laugh.

Luckily all my friends were from middle- or low-income families and for all of us (this was between 1985 and 1988), the hostel stay and food bills were affordable and cost-effective, providing great value for the money we had to pay. All three meals, breakfast, lunch and dinner, cost us only ₹12.00 per day, and one bed space, with two beds/persons per room, cost us only ₹75.00 per month.

Once the stressful period and tough exams were done with, we would all go and vacation in famous and popular tourist destinations such as the hill stations of Ooty and Kodaikanal or the famed beaches of Goa.

The CA course in India is probably the most inexpensive professional course in the world. We hardly spend anything for registration and also get a stipend during the articleship from the employer, which mostly covers all our expenses.

It was a fun place too. There were about 18–20 CA aspirants like me, and most of us qualified for the coveted degree while at CTC, quite a few passing with flying colours and moving to Dubai.

Even now when we get together for parties or connect over the telephone, we trade stories of those wonderful hostel days.

That reminds me of my fear of telephones while at U. Parasurama Iyer & Co.

Not having grown up with access to a telephone while in school and college, my constant exposure to the instrument began only when I started my articleship at the age of 22.

At the firm, which used to receive several calls during the day, sometimes I would be the only person free to answer the incoming calls, especially during lunch time, as most others would be otherwise engaged and would not be available to take the calls.

So when such a call came in, my heart would start racing and I would be in an anxious state, praying that someone would become free to receive the call.

This continued for a few weeks, after which, forced into handling many calls, I became an expert.

When I passed my intermediate exam—the first level of CA, which is followed by the final exam—I was carrying out an audit at the Centre for Water Resource Development and Management (CWRDM), Kunnamangalam, Kozhikode, a leading research and development institution in the water sector, established by the Government of Kerala.

I established a very good rapport with and was able to make a good impression on the Registrar and Accounts Officer. Because of that, I was offered a job there.

However, that did not materialize. Permanent posting in government jobs needs Public Service Commission approvals. I realized that it would be a very dangerous gamble and that I would have to risk my CA studies and articleship and, at the end of it, there was no surety that I would be selected.

So I did not take up the job.

Yet another incident that I remember from my auditing days at U. Parasurama Iyer & Co. makes me chuckle. Every morning, a CWRDM driver would pick me up from the CTC Hostel where I was staying, drive me to the institute about 15 kilometres away and then in the evening drop me back.

There were two drivers tasked with that. One was very polite, well-mannered, decent and always very punctual. The other was always arrogant, very rude, always late and sometimes even failed to turn up.

Since this was impacting my work schedule, I brought the driver's behaviour to the attention of the Accounts Officer, who in turn had some very harsh words for the truant.

This made the arrogant one even more furious with me and in a moment of anger, he burst into a tirade, shouting in the staff canteen and announcing to all present that he knew this boy who was used to waiting for hours to catch the only bus from Cheekilode that not only would halt often, to pick up people at every stop, but also all kinds of vegetables and lots of bananas, for which it would wait up to 15–20 minutes at every 3–4 stops, and now he had the gall to complain to the Officer that he was a few minutes late to pick him up.

One of the staff in the Accounts department told me about the driver's outburst. I found it quite amusing and told the Accounts staff that what he had said about the bus was true and that was precisely why I was keen that he picked me up on time, so that for a change I could also enjoy the ride in a comfortable and non-crowded government-sponsored car and reach my destination on time like an officer. I am sure that the Accounts department staff promptly passed this back to the driver.

A lot of us from the firm and the hostel—including Jose Mandoli, John, Vijayanand, Sathyanarayanan, Anitha, Jose, Boban, Kurian, Thankachan, Thomas, Charly, Sunny, Dilip, James, Augustine, Justine, Suresh, Abdu, Joy, Baby, Sajeevan, Haridas, Paulose, Sabu—are very good friends even now, maintaining close contact.

Of that glorious group of friends, 11 are now in Dubai, two in Qatar, one each in Austria, Canada and the US and five in India.

I fondly remember my good friends Jose Varghese Mandoli and Sajeevan, who are not with us anymore, and I pray that the Gods above give them eternal peace.

When on holiday in Kozhikode, I make it a point to catch up with those who are based in Kozhikode, Kerala and India.

CHAPTER **11**

A Palmist's Prophecy

Aʀᴍᴇᴅ ᴡɪᴛʜ ᴛʜᴇ ᴘʀᴇꜱᴛɪɢɪᴏᴜꜱ CA degree, I did what every new member of the renowned body would do before setting up on their own—get a suitable job with an equally reputed employer.

Those days, establishing a firm and practicing the trade was considered a prestigious affair and needed a bit of fixed capital, provision for operating expenses and good social and business networks to acquire a new business and sustain it.

And for getting suitable employment, there was a major obstacle: the lack of challenging, remunerative jobs.

In and around Kozhikode, not too many interesting jobs were available. Like most of Kerala at the time, there were very few reputed companies and hardly any multinationals. Most related jobs were with clay tile factories and trading setups, and they could not afford to pay a CA a decent salary, even if it was on the lower side.

I was not able to get a job of the kind that I had dreamt of during my CA days and that would keep me motivated. It was nowhere to be seen.

I was getting very frustrated.

It seemed to me that the only way to be meaningfully employed and earn some money was to set up a practice of my own, even if small.

In the meanwhile, I got an offer from my friend M. Dileep Kumar to join him as a partner in his firm M. Dileep Kumar & Company, Kozhikode, but after working together for a couple of months we realized that the practice was not big enough for two people.

Therefore, we decided to part ways, and the only option open to me was to start something of my own. I could not set up such an operation in Kozhikode. It would be prohibitively expensive.

I had to move into a small office space somewhere on the outskirts of the city.

After a bit of searching and networking, I found such a place in Thamarassery, about 30 kilometres or under an hour away from the city.

Thus in 1989 was born my first entrepreneurial venture, E.M. Rajagopalan & Company.

The move to Thamarassery was convenient because from there I could quickly reach the parallel college, College of English at Balussery, where I was teaching at that time, making around ₹1,000 (approximately US$62.00) per month.

I also used to teach at the same institute while I was studying for my M.Com.

So I would get on my bike, leave home, go to Balussery, complete the classes and then head to the firm.

The low rents, very limited operating expenses for running a small practice and easy access to the city made it a convenient and cost-effective start-up.

As I was a beginner, I roped in one of my B.Com students at the College of English, who was also a novice, to help me run the business. I faced all the teething troubles that a new, inexperienced, underfunded starter was bound to face.

We had great difficulty in handling things and we took much more time than normally required for clearing issues and matters with the tax department and other governmental departments that we had to interact with.

While I was practicing in Thamarassery, I had a client who ran liquor outlets—popularly referred to as bars in Kerala—and whose business was raided by a sales tax team to find if there were any tax evasions such as under-invoicing customers or even not invoicing at all to avoid paying dues to the government.

The matter was referred to me because I was handling their accounts. I went and met with the sales tax officer who was in charge of that particular case, a very unfriendly, arrogant guy who did not like CAs to go to the sales tax department because in his view getting bribes from CAs was a very difficult proposition.

This particular officer tried to negotiate with me for financial favours from the owner. I had even gone to his house to convince him against it.

But he was very adamant.

According to him he would return the favour by doctoring the case in such a way that the client would only have to pay a very small penalty to the government.

As a CA I did not want to deal with that kind of cheap, denigrating and illegal work. That case impacted my zeal.

It was a very uncomfortable, almost demeaning, shameful experience for me, and I hated doing this kind of middleman work for the seasoned businessman and this corrupt official.

My assistant, though only a B.Com student, was a very street-smart, crafty and devious operator. He made no effort to hide that part of his personality, which was obvious to all those who dealt with him, and cozied up to the client.

The client got a sense of the shrewd, manipulative nature of my deputy and in a cunning move, bypassed me and asked him to go and settle the matter with the officer.

Using his smooth-talking skills and wily ways, my junior handled the affair coolly. He ingratiated himself both with the client and the officer and negotiated a deal which was acceptable to both parties. He was very smug and aggressive about it.

That experience also made him overconfident and unabashedly brazen.

He thought that he could handle the clients and business all on his own, so he parted ways with me and poached all my clients in Thamarassery. He could do this because when we worked together, he would interface with clients while I did the real back-office work—no audit assignments but just bookkeeping and tax-related projects.

Broken and drained, I was staring emptily at the ceiling and at the busy road one day when out of the blue appeared a nomadic wayfarer who suddenly strode into the office.

She was a lean woman of around 50 years, carrying a small bamboo basket on her head and dressed in a red blouse and a beige *mundu*—a garment worn around the waist.

She said she was a palmist and could foresee the future and make predictions about it.

In Malayalam, we call such people *kakkathis* and their art is called *kainottam*.

At that time, I was not a believer, in anything. If at all I was a left-leaning atheist who believed in the power of money to help me better my life and living standards. I was sceptical about all such practices like palmistry and politely told her to go away.

But she was insistent, unwilling to give up.

Following her persistent, convincing requests, I gave in.

She took my hand, looked at the left palm very carefully for a long time and said that I would not be living in this land for long and that the best part of my life and future would be made elsewhere.

With the authority and confidence of a judge passing a verdict, she said, 'You will cross the seas. Next year when I am back here, you will not be in this office. You would have left this place, you would already have reached foreign lands.'

Once again, I told her I had no faith in palmistry or chirology or anything like that and that I did not quite believe what she had said. But I still paid more than what she had asked for as fees and forgot all about the incident.

Some events in life are very painful when they happen and we have to go through hell while they last, but when we look back at the timeline of life, they seem like blessings that triggered our move to much bigger, greater things.

And so was my entrepreneurial venture in Thamarassery, Kozhikode. What seemed a disaster then turned out to be a humungous blessing.

As I scan the files of my personal history while writing this book, I firmly believe that I experienced the disgraceful and excruciating phase for a reason, as per some divine design.

Otherwise, if that business had been successful, I would have been happy with the small fortune I was making in a place that was within my comfort zone. I would have been happily servicing unscrupulous clients and dealing with amoral bureaucrats and wasting my life in mediocrity.

This has happened to a lot of people. People got comfortable in their little successes and trapped by it for eternity, not able to realize their full potential.

To succeed and achieve one's maximum, a person has to take risks and venture out into the challenging world, the one outside their safe haven.

Enough was enough.

I decided to get out from my safe space and set out for the unknown.

I shut the practice immediately and within three months headed to Bombay. *Aamchi* Mumbai. Our Mumbai. It was to be my pit stop on the way to Dubai.

CHAPTER TWELVE

Mumbai (Bombay) Maze

For a lot of people from Kerala, of variegated backgrounds—the unfortunate, less educated but skilled workers, the professionals, the educated but less skilled workforce—who are desperate to build themselves a better life in a short time, the swiftest route is usually the Gulf, where the success rate is quite high.

All Gulf Co-operation Council (GCC) economies, except Kuwait, are pegged to the US Dollar and the purchasing power parities of most countries are significantly higher in the GCC as compared to the country of origin of the expatriate workers.

Not that all migrant workers are successful. Many have fallen by the wayside despite their best efforts. Some have made it big despite being less than average.

I was not a believer in a higher force, a divine, guiding spiritual power that chaperones one to success, but after looking back at my own story, I am now not a disbeliever.

For I have felt that divine blessing, as have so many million foreign workers over the years.

Most Keralites and Indians often have an intermediary stop on the way from their states while on their journey to the shores of Arabia. For a lot of aspirants, especially those from rural backgrounds, this would be a halt at a town or city in their own state, followed by a pit stop at the nearest metro, mostly Mumbai or Delhi to arm oneself with the equipment required to survive the relentless, gruelling tests in the Gulf. (Mumbai was still Bombay when I stayed there for a year. The anglicized name was replaced with its Marathi counterpart in 1995 by the Shiv Sena. The English had gained possession of the city in the seventeenth century, and the Portuguese name Bombaim—meaning 'good little bay' in Portuguese—was anglicized to Bombay.)

It was not too different for me either.

Starting from Edavilangu, Kodungallur, it had been a voyage crisscrossing many villages and towns and cities—Kadungallur, Aricode, Kizhisserry, Cheekilode, Chelannur, Madappally—until I finally reached the limit of my upwardly movement in Kozhikode and by then was sure that if I wanted to scale up the ladder quickly I would, inevitably, have to land up in Dubai, or else be eternally confined to my current life situation, surviving and able to meet my needs but never ever reach the levels of comfort and ostentatiousness I saw a lot of my friends and neighbours enjoy.

I had to go to Dubai.

In preparation and to get the gear and fuel needed to sustain me in Dubai, I needed one last stopover, an essential one, to pick up my gladiatorial must for that race of a lifetime.

There were two things missing in my armoury: work experience with a multinational brand and finer communication skills in English. To fill those gaps, I had decided to head to Mumbai. The maximum city. The only one in India that never sleeps.

With that aim in mind, I reached out to my friend Charly from the CTC Hostel, who by now was settled in his job with PricewaterhouseCoopers in Bombay.

As expected, he agreed to help me out, facilitating my comfortable stay in Mumbai.

So, in September 1990, after celebrating Onam at home as is customary, I set out for Bombay by train—I distinctly remember it was a Thursday—and reached the vibrant city on Sunday. Charly and some of the friends with whom he was staying received me at Dadar railway station, one of the main stops for long distance trains from across India.

All of us piled into an iconic black and yellow Premier Padmini taxi and drove up to CGS Colony, Antop Hill, which was to be my home for that one-year stay in Bombay.

To equip myself for Dubai, I was very keen to get a job with a reputed firm.

Luckily, without too much of a search, I got a job with the very well-known and respected auditing and consulting firm A.F. Ferguson & Co., Chartered Accountants, Fort, Bombay. This was the oldest accounting firm in India, which later integrated its operations with one of the largest global audit firms, Deloitte Haskins & Sells (DH&S) in 2004.

At the historic firm I was to work with the team under partners Mr K.M. Pawala and Mr F. M. Chinoy and managers Mr Shyam Tata and Mr Verma.

The office was in the Allahabad Bank building, Mumbai Samachar Marg, Kala Ghoda, Fort, the central business district of India's commercial capital.

To cover the distance from our residence in Antop Hill to Fort, Charly and I would take the suburban train. As it was always packed to the hilt, and we had to get to the office in a presentable state, we would travel by first class, which was relatively inexpensive and less crowded.

Work at the office was very methodical and formal, but most of the assignments included auditing at the clients' office.

There were some memorable incidents, too.

In my Fort office, I had an office manager who was also a CA and whose name was Mr Sanghvi.

Having woken up late following the earlier night's partying and hangover, I would sometimes be late to get to work by an hour or so. I would therefore miss the timings allotted for each person to complete their morning ablutions.

Most of the time, I would sneak quietly into the office to avoid being seen by Mr Sanghvi and most of the time would get away with the crime.

But sometimes I would get caught.

If he spotted me coming in late, he would demand an explanation in his booming voice: 'Rajagopal, where were you?'

In a very submissive and polite tone, I would tell him that I had to wash my clothes in the morning and that was why I was late.

Being the kind and understanding man that he was, he would readily accept the story with a soft warning not to repeat it again.

If not on audit duty with clients, being a little late did not impact my work and output at all. While at the Fort office, we never had desk work and would be idling in the office, discussing worldly matters and gossiping about office politics. Most of the work was client-centric and took place at clients' offices and factories.

When we did not have work, we were supposed to go to the office to fill the time sheet of non-chargeable engagement.

So, after work, unlike in many countries where colleagues catch up for a drink or coffee, in Bombay, the race to get back home begins.

While working in Fort, there was not much time to enjoy the many small eateries around the area. The priority was to catch the earliest possible train to avoid the maddening rush of people in a crazy haste to get home after work. But while on audit assignments, the generous clients, always willing to please the auditors, would often take us to the best restaurants around and thereby I got to see, taste and enjoy some of the best dining places in Bombay.

Like in CTC Hostel, my apartment mates at CGS Colony— Central Government Employees' Society Colony, popularly known as CGS Colony, is one of Asia's largest housing colonies, providing housing to employees and staff of central government bodies/organizations based in the city—Antop Hill, K.S. Charly, Joepaul, Sojen Manjila, Benny, Paul Manjila, Gangadharan, Augustine, Rafi and Ramakrishnan, made for a fun gang.

As with a lot of Keralites, having fun involves a bit of alcohol, and our gang was no different. We would regularly have informal parties at home and on occasions slip into Neelam Bar to have some more fun. Once in a while we would also frequent a cheap bar which was known for its local brew.

Bombay is known for its street food. *Vada pav, panipuri, bhelpuri, sevpuri, dahipuri, sandwiches, ragda-pattice, pav bhaji...* there was a wide variety to choose from. On weekends we would go to the popular tourist spots of Bombay, Chowpatty Beach, Colaba, Fort, etc. and taste the fantastic variety on offer.

Bombay is a magical place. It is very crowded and noisy, with people jostling with each other for everything; yet in a strange way things work like clockwork.

Bombay amazed me in many things. For somebody from a small Kerala village, watching the sheer number of people in Fort station and how they moved in waves was a stunning experience initially.

In the morning, with each train dropping off people at the station, there would be wave after wave of huge multitudes pouring out of the various exits, as if in a choreographed move, heading in the areas and directions that would take them to their intended destinations. So some would make a beeline for the next bus stop and some for the nearest taxi rank, while others set out on a spirited, brisk walk to their journey's end.

At every stage there is competition, there is an element of a struggle for survival.

That city can make anyone aggressive. It is a living university, a training ground which proves Charles Darwin's 'survival of the fittest' theory every day through the practical of life.

Whether one needs to buy a newspaper or a cigarette, unless a desperate, combative push is made to get to the head of the line, those who are meek and submissive in nature will find themselves pushed back to the last in no time.

On the other hand, for more formal things, there would be a very organized, patient queue.

So while waiting for the BEST (Brihanmumbai Electric Supply & Transport) buses—the iconic red and silver workhorses that ply on Bombay roads along with the black and yellow cabs—or when buying railway tickets or waiting in a shared taxi line, the discipline and orderliness of the queue systems really amazed me.

Everyone has to compete for everything and that instils a sense of combativeness that equips people with the necessary assertiveness and inventiveness required to survive in a Darwinian dog-eat-dog world.

And that is often perceptible and visible in people hailing from that crucible of contests, that cauldron of combats, *Aamchi* Mumbai.

As with every village, town and city, Bombay also has its seamy, slimy side.

Crime is rampant, but I have been very lucky not to have been impacted in any way, even by a petty crime such as pickpocketing, which is a major issue. I was very lucky not to lose my purse even once throughout my stay in Bombay. Not too many people are this fortunate.

Not having been aware about the existence of *hijras*—transgender and intersex people—I was very surprised to see them on Bombay's streets and traffic intersections in their shimmering saris, their faces heavily made up with cheap cosmetics, knocking on car windows for alms and in turn offering blessings.

With each day ticking by, a blessing no doubt, the time allotted for my stay in that city was edging closer to the end.

It felt as if I was being pushed on by the palmist's prophecy. I began to accelerate the process of my departure to Dubai.

CHAPTER THIRTEEN

Prophecy Comes True

M<small>Y ORIGINAL PLAN</small> A was shaping up well.

I had gained the work experience and communication prowess required, giving me the confidence to move to Dubai on a visit visa to check out the opportunities.

Plan B? If I was not successful, I would return to Bombay.

The precarious state of the Indian economy, with all key economic numbers and indicators plunging to an embarrassing nadir in the summer of 1991, when the country had no other option but to pledge its national reserve of gold to obtain a life-giving, face-saving loan from the International Monetary Fund (IMF), was making the prospects of employment and a lucrative future grim.

Later, transformative reforms came as India grappled with one of its darkest economic chapters ever.

The 1991 Indian economic crisis resulted from poor economic policies pursued over the years and the resultant trade deficits.

India's economic problems started worsening in 1985 as the imports swelled, leaving the country in a twin deficit: the Indian trade balance was in deficit at a time when the government was running on a huge fiscal deficit.

By the end of 1990, in the run-up to the Gulf War, the dire situation meant that the Indian foreign exchange reserves could have barely financed three weeks' worth of imports.

Meanwhile, the government came close to defaulting on its own financial obligations.[4]

By July that year, the low reserves had led to a sharp depreciation of the rupee, which in turn exacerbated the twin deficit problem. The Chandra Shekhar government could not pass the budget in February 1991 after Moody downgraded India's bond ratings.

The ratings further deteriorated due to the unsuccessful passage of the fiscal budget. This made it impossible for the country to seek short-term loans and aggravated the existing economic crisis. The World Bank and IMF also stopped their assistance, leaving the government with no option but to mortgage the country's gold to avoid defaulting on payments.

In an attempt to seek an economic bailout from the IMF, the Indian government airlifted its national gold reserves.

The crisis, in turn, paved the way for the liberalization of the Indian economy, since one of the conditions stipulated in the World Bank loan—structural reform—required India to open itself up to participation from foreign entities in its industries, including its state-owned enterprises.

---

4   Wikipedia: The Free Encyclopedia. '1991 Indian Economic Crisis.' Available at https://en.wikipedia.org/wiki/1991_Indian_economic_crisis.

It was clear that I had to leave India.

From A.F. Ferguson, I had earned my multinational brand badge. As a result of working at that firm and living in Mumbai, my English communication skills had been honed to the level I wanted. The twin objectives of Mission Mumbai were achieved in the one year that I had earmarked for them.

As planned, I resigned from A.F. Ferguson after a year of service, which I had completed in the first week of October.

In November, after the sweltering hot, sultry, searing heat of summer has subsided, the weather in Dubai turns splendid with the onset of winter, with glorious, breezy, cool, dry days heralding the countdown to the last two months of the year.

It is the ideal climate and the business clime, too, is perfect as it marks the beginning of the hiring season also, when organizations ready their businesses to take on the challenges of the new year.

That is the right time to land in Dubai, especially for job hunters who have to do a lot of moving around, meeting up with prospective employers, networking and attending interviews.

It was time to move to the final destination. The City of Gold. The City of Dreams. Dubai. The palmist's prediction was coming true.

CHAPTER FOURTEEN

Muziris To Dubai

For decades, DUBAI AND UAE have been a succour, a lodestar, a dream and a saviour for several Keralites.

There was this strong conviction, this unshakable faith that once you get to that fabled land, by dint of hard work and the fruits of your labour, there would be success at the end, a glorious light at the end of the tunnel.

And the Dubai Dream came right in time for Kerala.

The sixties were tumultuous years for one of the most developed and progressive states. Though it boasted of the highest literacy levels in India, its per capita income was one of the lowest.

The state was frequently witnessing intense political tussles between the Communists, who had created history of sorts by making the party and the state become one of the first in the world to be democratically elected to power, forming a government in the late 1950s, and the Indian National Congress, which was in power in most Indian states at that time.

A frustrated breakaway set of Communists, the Naxalites, were also very active in the hilly districts of northern Kerala.

Newspapers were regularly full of stories of decapitations, police raids and a terrorized populace.

India too was in the throes of its birth pangs.

After a decades-long fight for Independence, the nation had become free on 15 August 1947, but it was a country made up of 571 disjointed princely states which was then sifted and filtered to create 27 states, thereby causing incessant strife and unrest all along.

And as things were settling down came the disastrous war with China, with its collateral damage to various spheres of Indian life. All this trickled down into Kerala as well.

The state's finances were in trouble, there was not too much food going around, the educated, healthy young of the state did not have meaningful employment and into this boiling cauldron were added the violent political movements causing further disarray in the ranks of the people.

Kerala and its people needed an escape valve. And that came in the form of Dubai, UAE and the Gulf countries.

Dubai too was a quiet fishing hamlet, with trade centred around the creek being the mainstay.

By the 1960s, Dubai's economy was driven mostly by revenues from trade and, to a smaller extent, oil exploration concessions, but oil was not discovered until 1966. Oil revenue first started to flow in 1969. The oil revenue helped accelerate the early development of the city, but its reserves are limited and production levels are low: Today, less than 5 per cent of the revenue comes from oil.

Dubai, right across the Arabian Sea, is now just a quick hop away by plane. But in those early days of migration, people mostly travelled there illegally by rough-hewn boats and vessels variously known as *pathemaris* (dhows) and *urus*. Early migrants to the Gulf from Kerala thus embarked on a clueless, dangerous journey in search of escape, often on a wing and a prayer and the mercy of the seas and the winds.

Many perished while on that adventurous yearning for a livelihood, but many more waded to those shores to find a job, mostly menial and physically intensive hard work, but work that nevertheless provided sustenance to them and their families back home.

With the construction boom in the late sixties, the trickle of adventurous migration gave way to a more legal, less dangerous and conventional mode of exodus of labour as Keralites already in the Gulf began getting in more of their friends and relatives to benefit from the magnanimity of the land, its rulers and people.

Thus began the furthering of trade and relations that have been around from the times of Muziris when traders from Arabia would come into Kerala to buy spices in exchange for the incense and such goods they possessed.

The story of Muziris starts from early 3000 BC when Babylonians, Assyrians and Egyptians came to the Malabar Coast in search of the spices. Later, these Middle Eastern groups were joined by Arabs and Phoenicians. And gradually, Muziris in Kodungallur entered into the cartography of World trade map. Then onwards Muziris holds the key to a good chunk of Kerala's ancient history and now the ancient trade route.

So given the backdrop of job opportunities available, the extant entrepreneurial ecosystem and the dreams for a much better life, quite early on it was firmly implanted that all my education, experiences and skills would provide many more opportunities and fetch much more returns in Dubai.

I had made up my mind to make my fortunes in Dubai.

And I decided to try the tested and proven route—get a visit visa through a relative, try it out for three months, find a job and return if I failed.

And try again.

Round One.

I called up my cousin Syamasundaran Chettan (Chettan is a respectful way of addressing an elder brother in Malayalam), who was also from Kodungallur and was working with Port Rashid in Dubai, and sought his help to get a visit visa.

The forever helpful Chettan did it in record time and also proffered his hospitality in Dubai while I hunted for a job.

Dubai beckoned.

I heeded the call.

CHAPTER FIFTEEN

Dazzling Dubai

IT WAS MY FIRST flight ever.

After 29 years of traversing mostly in Kerala and then in Mumbai by road and rail, for the first time in my life I was taking a flight.

I toyed with the idea of going home to Cheekilode to bid farewell to my family but having spent time with them during that Onam—with Thiruvonam falling on 23 August—and extending my stay into September for a holiday, I decided against it. I had returned to Bombay only a few weeks earlier.

Onam is an annual harvest festival celebrated in Kerala by people of all three major religions—Hinduism, Islam and Christianity—each of which has a billion followers worldwide who have been coexisting in a remarkable show of tolerance and peace for centuries.

Legends say that the festival is celebrated to commemorate King Mahabali, whose spirit is said to visit Kerala at the time of Onam.

On 7 November 1991, I boarded the flight from Mumbai. And befittingly, it was an Emirates flight.

There was no apprehension, just excitement.

After a couple of drinks in a toast of sorts to that dream destination and a few cigarettes at the back of the cabin, as smoking had not yet been banned on flights, the landing announcement was heard through the PA system. The short, three-hour flight was almost over.

The first sights of the City of Dreams came into view as the plane circled over the airport while landing, and a mixture of emotions flooded my mind.

I experienced the exploratory glee of arriving in a new yet very familiar place, a city and country about which every Keralite dreams. I was unsure of what the future held even though I had very clear visions of what it should be.

I wanted my life in the new haven to be as starkly, vibrantly different from the airport I had just left behind.

The energy at the airport, if it is any indicator of the zing of the city, was quite infectious.

There was a buzz that in some ways injected hope and courage in a new, apprehensive yet confident entrant wishing to play in its competitive fields, determined to make a serious play of it.

The bright lights, orderly queues, well-laid-out procedures, efficient counters, the cleanliness of the airport, steely determination of most passengers, whether residents or those on business or leisure, each aware that they were here on a mission, and the no-nonsense approach of all once again reminded me that I had to play by a new set of rules that I was probably not used to in the vast jungle of a city that I had left behind.

I had a hunch that I was on to something completely new, something completely different, something big.

I was almost fully confident that with my educational accomplishments, academic achievements and work experience, I would be able to get a good job.

Plan B, at the very back of my mind, was the confidence that if I did not get a job during this visit, I would go back to Mumbai, find a job there or again come back for another try.

It was comforting to see my cousin Syamasundaran Chettan waiting to receive me. It was reassuring that I was not alone in this strange land and that I could always count on Chettan to prop me up if I had a bad day.

The orderly lines for taxis was a new experience for me and so was the diligent driving of the cabbie and the disciplined ride during which I was quite stunned to see all the vehicles following the traffic rules to a T.

After a short drive, we reached Chettan's residence near the Falcon Roundabout in Bur Dubai, which was to be my haven for the next few weeks. On the way I could see the gleaming lights of the City of Gold, tall towers shining like guiding lighthouses of commerce, swanky cars rolling away into the night and exchanging lanes in a swift act of acceleration, gliding from the slow to the fast lane with ease.

I made a note of all that.

I had planned my visit to coincide with winter, a great time to be in Dubai.

Chettan had warned about the scorching heat of summer and how it might not be the best time for those seeking a job to be landing in the city.

All excited about being in a new place and very keen to survey the setting and, most importantly, explore the job opportunities, I woke up early the following day and set out on a short walk.

What Chettan had said was true.

There was a nip in the air, and a slight breeze made the walk very pleasant. As I stepped out of the apartment building, very close to Falcon Roundabout, which was built in the 1970s, at the junction of Al Mina Road, Bank Street and Al Ghubaiba Road, and walked a short distance, there rose before me a grandiose statue of a majestic bird perched in the eye of the large, well-manicured, grassy roundabout, scanning with scrutiny for the next opportunity.

It was not difficult to understand why the falcon was the national bird of the UAE.

The regal bird, with its stately posture, soaring flight and quicksilver reflexes, has historically been a prized possession of the Bedouin, at once representing survival, training, honour and sportsmanship.

It reminded me that in a way I was similarly perched. Waiting for the right opportunity. I walked on.

Used to seeing just three or four models of cars in the villages and towns of Kerala—Ambassador, Fiat which later became Premier Padmini, Standard Herald and then in the eighties the Maruti—and then the occasional foreign car in Calicut and Mumbai, I was stunned to see the range of cars on the road there.

After a quick survey of the surroundings, I enthusiastically walked back to the apartment situated near Palm Beach Hotel to begin my job search in earnest.

The falcon does not waste time. In Dubai nobody does. You move fast to win.

CHAPTER SIXTEEN

The Hunt Begins

Back THEN IN NOVEMBER 1991, at the time of fax and landlines and just as mobile phones were becoming popular, the job vacancies available were to be found predominantly through personal networking, the appointments columns in the two prominent English newspapers *Khaleej Times* and *Gulf News* and through the few recruiting agencies.

I tried all means possible, predominantly relying on the appointments columns of newspapers.

By this time, I had also established contacts with some of my CA friends from Kozhikode and Bombay who were already in Dubai.

I kept applying, hearing back from some companies, meeting with radio silence from others and being called for interviews by a few.

I guess I attended around six interviews—one with a supermarket chain, another with a multinational logistics company—before I got a call from the kind of employer I preferred: an audit firm that went by the name of Mohammed Abdul Karim & Partners (Mak & Partners).

The Founder and Group Managing Partner, Mr Khalid Maniar, himself interviewed me. Even while being very modest, I must admit that I had quite an impressive CV.

I had cleared both groups of the Chartered Accountancy exams conducted by ICAI in one attempt, a rare feat for candidates appearing for the prestigious course conducted by the ICAI which has 'achieved recognition as a premier accounting body not only in the country but also globally, for maintaining highest standards in technical, ethical areas and for sustaining stringent examination and education standards. Since 1949, the profession has grown leaps and bounds in terms of members and student base'.[5]

Additionally, I was the topper and gold medalist at the Kozhikode (also known by its English adaptation Calicut) branch of the ICAI and had won the T.R. Subramanya Iyer Memorial Cash Award of ₹250.00 (around US$15.00 then) for the same.

Moreover, I had gained a multinational brand experience through my one-year stint at A.F. Ferguson in Bombay and was now confident of my English communications skills, which I had honed over time at various workplaces, particularly India's commercial capital.

Mr Maniar interviewed me for about an hour, mostly probing me to get insights into my attitude and my compatibility with the workplace.

---

5   The Institute of Chartered Accountants of India (ICAI). Available at https://icai.org/new_post.html?post_id=165.

My academic achievements, professional qualifications and the various certificates were neatly laid out in front of him as he kept questioning me more and more—about my character, my disposition to work challenges and my affability.

He was amply satisfied and at the end of the one hour of prodding and probing, although done in quite the friendly, avuncular, gracious and polite manner of discussions for which I admired Mr Maniar, and which for me became a hallmark that I was quick to adapt as my communication style with my peers, subordinates, colleagues and staff, he gave me the nod.

It was one of the many lessons that I learned from Khalid Bhai, as I would call him respectfully while interacting with him when I worked at Mak & Partners and even later.

With a friendly yet strong clasp, he shook my hand and welcomed me into the organization.

As there were no CAs at the firm when I joined, I was appointed the Audit Manager.

I was thrilled that I had landed the kind of job I was keen on. I was proud of the designation granted. The salary was good, around AED3,500, which when converted then was around ₹23,310.

It was quite a fortune compared to my last salary with A.F. Fergusson, which had been ₹2,750.

I could not contain my glee. I called up Syamasundaran Chettan first and then Achan and Amma to convey the great news.

We were all thrilled.

I was beginning to like Dubai.

I learned from my friends a little later that India, after the national ignominy of 1991 (when due to the crippling state of the Indian economy there had been massive unemployment and double-digit inflation, the public debt had stood at 55 per cent of GDP, the nation's foreign exchange reserves had dipped to a point where it could only support imports for another two weeks and the government was forced to mortgage the country's gold to avoid defaulting on payments) and pursuant liberalization of the economy, things had turned positive very quickly, and there was a massive hike in their salaries from ₹2,750 (US$106) to ₹11,000 (US$425) in Ferguson.

I joined my new workplace by early December 1991 and within the same month I got my first salary in Dubai.

Out of the ₹23,310, I sent ₹19,000 to my mother, a very princely sum at that time because the exchange rate was less than ₹10 to an Emirati Dirham.

Having spent the major chunk of my first salary on the remittance home, I saved the rest for my conveyance (an allowance for that was part of the salary and I could not claim for my commutes) and living expenses.

Having found a decent job of my liking with a good salary, I thought it was not right to burden Syamasundaran Chettan anymore and not overstay his hospitality. Therefore, I decided to move in with my close friends from my CA days in Kozhikode, Boban, Thankachan and his wife Sholy, his sister Jessy and her husband Salu, who were staying in a two-bedroom apartment on Yousuf Baker Road, just off Nasser Square in Deira.

The move was celebrated in style at the new residence.

It was very close to the Mak & Partners office in Al Ghurair Apartment, under 20 minutes by walk or 6–8 minutes by taxi.

I would mostly take a taxi ride, ready to spend a little and reach very fresh to the office than walk in sweaty and tired.

When spending and investment are needed, I do not hold back. I open up my purse, judiciously.

With an exciting job, a good salary and my visa formalities completed—employment visa stamped on my passport after the completion of all due processes—by February 1992, I had regularized my stay in Dubai.

Now I had officially become a Gulfee, as non-resident Indians working in the Gulf Cooperation Council (GCC) countries are commonly referred to in Kerala.

The first part of my Dubai dream had come true.

CHAPTER SEVENTEEN

The First Break

LIFE AND WORK AT Mak & Partners were a big learning curve.

Khalid Bhai was a father figure and I picked up a lot of lessons by observing him.

My office was just a short walk away from one of the historic centres of the city in Deira.

Initially, I was engaged predominantly in audit, but I was also involved with feasibility studies, business plans and associated matters, which were part of the consulting services offered by the organization. There was no separate consulting division at the time.

I was very good at the work.

Among the many lessons that I learned from Khalid Bhai, there was one I particularly incorporated into my work style at the firm and even later as a cardinal principle. That was giving the staff the freedom to work, allowing enough leeway for them to work at their own pace, with flexible timings, not micromanaging and interfering in their assignments and tasks as long as the quality and quantity of output was achieved within the agreed deadline.

I would also ensure that all staff working with me had the required tools, facilities and support needed to deliver.

As with the interview process, in which Khalid Bhai had continuously checked to get a measure of my attitude, when I recruit people for my office, I usually do a one-hour interview during which I judge the attitude of the interviewee.

For I have learnt that the quality of a person's work can be shaped and improved provided the person has the right disposition.

Attitude encompasses a whole array of qualities, including the attitude towards the work, the manner in which a client is treated, work ethics, integrity, the approach to tackling severe work pressure, the general temperament and how unflappable a person is under adverse situations, handling of peers and also, very importantly, the respect proffered to subordinates.

I also learnt that within the span of an hour available for a candidate interview, scrutinizing all the above requisites might not be possible, but by adhering to my thumb rule I have, over the years, had a success rate of around 70 per cent in analysing people accurately.

Hard work was the cardinal principle for me. And what I look for in my people, too.

I was putting in a lot of hard work. I did not look at the clock and restrict the time available for work but using the flexibility given to me by my boss and, without putting any time limits, strove hard to ensure that I contributed to the organization.

That is also the kind of dedication that I look for in people joining my organization. I look for those who utilize the opportunity given to gain knowledge, experience and enrich themselves, and thereby the institution, career-wise and financially, rather than spend time on shirking work to accumulate more educational qualifications.

With a single-minded focus on bettering the organization's reputation and revenue and thereby, through trickle-down benefits, improving my financial situation, I was doing well.

Khalid Bhai was happy. And he was willing to give me freer rein. And I was still observing him and learning.

As part of his appreciation of the work that I was doing and as a token of his willingness to acknowledge that and incentivize me to produce more for the company, I was made a partner in 1995.

It meant that along with a salary and new designation, I was given a 12.5 per cent share of the profit which, after three years, would increase to 17.5 per cent.

I was passionate about my job and my boss was extremely confident that I could create significant additional value to the practice if properly compensated. And so I was considered a good prospect for the promotion.

One of my boss's greatest traits was to try out new things, albeit with limited risks and exposure.

So, as if through some divine blessing, a significant pivotal turn in life came in the form of such a venture. It was as if some force above was guiding the course of my life.

I was never a great believer in God or an observer of religious rituals or customs.

Maybe, on the contrary, I was an agnostic and atheist, primarily because Achan had leftist leanings and never believed in God or religion and Amma was too busy with work and children to have the time for regular temple visits or observances, although she was not a disbeliever.

With that as the backdrop, none of us kids were overly religious, and me, owing to the overwhelming left leanings of the places that I grew up in, I was more aligned to being a sceptic.

But later, the events of my life would compel me to believe that there is a powerful force above covering me with its protection and blessing me in generous abundance.

There were many such incidents.

Though I did not realize it then, or become a believer, the new opportunity that Khalid Bhai took on and passed on to me was a game changer.

Like many things in life, as they say, this also happened with a small step. I had come to Dubai and joined Mak & Partners at the right time.

CHAPTER EIGHTEEN

The Big Break

IN THE EARLY 1990S, there was a particular vibrancy in the business circles of the UAE, especially Dubai.

Dubai's strategic vision of garnering a share of the global shipping, logistics and allied businesses, and at the same time, developing its own manufacturing and industrial capabilities was given a boost by the success of the Jebel Ali Free Zone in 1985.

It was the culmination of the vision and dream of the late Sheikh Rashid bin Saeed Al-Maktoum, then ruler of Dubai.

In the late 1960s and early 1970s, it was felt that the port of Dubai, Port Rashid, could not meet the growing demands of the city and the nation and did not have any scope for further expansion because of its location within the city.

So Jebel Ali, 35 kilometres southwest of Dubai, by the coast parallel to the road to Abu Dhabi, would be the location for the new, state-of-the-art deepwater port.

Construction began in the early 1970s and was completed in 1979. The port was inaugurated by Queen Elizabeth II on 26 February 1979.

Now Jebel Ali is one of the world's top ten busiest ports, boasts of the largest man-made harbour and is the biggest and by far the busiest port in the Middle East.

With a massive deepwater port capable of handling huge ships and volumes and designed to drive a quantum growth in business, Jebel Ali Port became a free zone in 1980 after a year of operation. At that point, the only distinguishing characteristic of a free zone was that it was a customs-free zone for re-exports.

Recognizing the potential of the free zone to be capable of driving much more business than what it was doing, in 1985, the Jebel Ali Free Zone Authority (JAFZA) was established as an independent authority to manage the growth of JAFZ into a regional and global player.

The very next year, in 1986, the free zone became independent of Dubai municipal laws and by 1992, allied business ventures that would benefit and thrive in the new ecosystem—termed Free Zone Establishments (FZEs), they were limited to one shareholder—could be incorporated to allow for independent business inside the free zone.

In 1998, the UAE Commercial Companies Law was amended to carve out the free zones, allowing establishment of Free Zone Companies (FZCOs) inside JAFZ.

When JAFZA was set up in 1985, it had around 19 companies. In a decade's time, the number had swelled to more than 500. Now, three decades later, it has over 8,000 companies, including nearly 100 Fortune Global 500 enterprises.

Now JAFZA is a globally connected dynamic hub for thousands of businesses from over 100 countries, accounts for around 24 per cent of Dubai's foreign direct investment and provides employment to more than 135,000 people from all over the world.

With huge markets of the wider Middle East region comprising West Asia and the Commonwealth of Independent States (CIS), Africa and the Indian subcontinent within an easy, well-connected radius, a lot of companies have set up their regional headquarters in JAFZ to gain access to and service the bilateral, multilateral and remunerative transit trades from these geographies.

Back then, JAFZ, almost at the outer periphery of Dubai on the coast and along the narrow road to Abu Dhabi, was expanding at a hectic pace.

Its connectivity to the hinterland also got a major boost as the UAE roads infrastructure was being given major upgrades with the construction of new highways and bridges and widening of existing roads.

Business was booming.

In 1996, our enterprise would flourish too.

In early 1996, identifying an opportunity, an Emirati national, a lady by the name of Ms Safiya Haji Akbar Mohammed, who had an audit business and licence which was not being utilized properly, approached Khalid Bhai through one of her employees based on the reputation being developed by Mak & Partners. She sought to rejuvenate the business.

Never one to say no to new opportunities, Khalid Bhai gladly accepted the challenge and, by virtue of the trust and confidence that he had in me, promptly asked me to start a new venture under the new licence.

The name of the company as per the trade licence was Certain Audit Bureau.

With the licence and the business came another possession, a small office on top of Hadeer Supermarket on Al Rasheed Road in the Hor Al Anz area of Deira in Dubai.

As per the business arrangements, systems and procedures prevalent then, as the UAE national sponsor, Ms Mohammed was to be paid a fixed sum, and the net profit was to be shared by the three partners of the new company: Khalid Bhai would get a 40 per cent share, I would get a salary of AED7,500 plus housing, a car and 40 per cent share, and another partner working with Mak & Partners would get the remaining 20 per cent.

Just after completing three exciting years with Mak & Partners, during which I learnt about business, business development, management and creating value, I moved out of that company to run the newly created entity, although certain privileges such as my signing rights and visa were still with Mak & Partners.

In April 1996, I was in charge of resuscitating Certain Audit Bureau, giving it a new lease of life.

I employed a couple of staff for handling clerical work at the existing office, who would not cost too much in terms of salaries. I also hired Ikram Ahmed, a Pakistani boy, to handle the visa-, labour- and administration-related matters, a role commonly and curiously called Public Relations Officer, a terminology usually associated with media.

The new office was given a thorough cleaning, and we were in business.

True to Khalid Bhai's style of working, which I learnt from him and emulated all through my career, he did not support me with any work assignments but gave me full freedom to develop my own business, which I did with support from my staff.

I am sure that had I requested him for help, he would never have said no.

But I liked the freedom and independence to work on my own, and that is exactly how I function even today. I hire the right people and give them full freedom to develop and deliver.

I had to toil hard, on my own, very well supported by a collaborative team.

We were successful in the very first month, breaking even in the initial 30 days, mainly because the expenses, including my salary, were very minimal. And there was no debt burden as none of the partners had contributed capital.

By the end of the sixth or seventh month, Certain Audit Bureau paid back the AED7,500 which the boss had paid to the sponsor, and when the books were closed at the end of the first year, our maiden year, we were making a profit of around AED200,000. The profits were shared as agreed.

While Certain Audit Bureau was consolidating its reach and business, Khalid Bhai and his team were doing their own empire-building at an intense pace.

With the UAE economy booming, Khalid Bhai envisioned that to capitalize on the opportunities and scale up quickly, Mak & Partners required a global identity to make more inroads into the market and tap into the international businesses being established in the country.

Therefore, the organization joined AGN International (then CKL International), a worldwide association of separate and independent accounting and consulting firms. The company was rebranded as AGN MAK.

Needing more space to accommodate the additional workforce joining the firm to handle the new business, Khalid Bhai and AGN MAK decided to move from the Gargash Centre office in the midst of the bustling Nasser Square area of Deira—to which he had moved from the first office in the Al Ghurair Apartment—to a much posher building, Reem Tower, on the iconic Al Maktoum Street, a stone's throw away from the landmark Clock Tower built in 1965 and popular through its photographic reproduction in innumerable global books, magazines, publications, websites and social media platforms.

As I have mentioned repeatedly, I used to watch him at work, observing the way he deftly handled matters, and learnt a lot about strategic business moves and their timely implementation.

With Certain Audit Bureau also strategizing to make the most of the burgeoning business in Dubai and the UAE in general, I decided to move to a larger office space (and dreamt of a rebrand). By then we had also grown slightly and had a staff strength of five.

So it was kind of poetic and poignant that I would follow my guru and move into the Gargash Centre office vacated by Khalid Bhai in December 1997.

It already had enough office space with ready shelving units and cabins and could accommodate more people if the business so warranted.

And it was time to come out of the shadows of the father-like master and create my own space, a lesson he himself taught me by example.

It was certain that Certain Audit Bureau had to get a new moniker.

With both businesses expanding significantly, there were some profound professional differences of opinion between me and the boss. I was grateful to him for all his help and, not wanting to continue as an unhappy and disgruntled partner, I began to consider starting something completely on my own.

For the boy from that thatched hut in Kodungallur, almost 2,800 kilometres from home as the jet flies, in sunny Dubai, an unexpected twist in life, another turn for greater success, was around the corner.

CHAPTER NINETEEN

A God's Gift, by the Banks of the River Mayyazhi

I HAD A GREAT BOSS and was thoroughly enjoying my work and the workplace. At the end of long and tiring days, I would come to a warm and friendly residence, with very close friends providing an absolutely fun, relaxing environment.

We used to have mirthful nights on Thursdays, weekends and holidays, with a lot of political discussions, reminiscing of life back home, Malayalam movies and often music and singing, even if it was all sadly out of tune and harmony.

Although I had kind of settled down, at the back of my mind there was always a gnawing longing to find a wife—someone like Amma who was kind, humane, empathetic, hardworking and would complement me—have a family, set up a warm nest and enjoy its cosiness.

The year which had begun on an exciting note continued that way.

I was enjoying the work and was greatly satisfied and happy that I could generously take care of the affairs of home and allied expenses. And life in the apartment was fun.

A year went by in a flash.

As I was completing my first year, Khalid Bhai sanctioned my annual leave, and I was scheduled to travel home in late November.

At that point, I was nearly 30 years old, eager to get married and turn over a new page in my life.

Or should I wait until I had settled down into a very peaceful frame of mind before tying the knot?

That would have meant that another two years would go by. But I weighed all options very objectively, considered all the pros and cons and decided that everything would be fine.

The cordial work atmosphere, the possibilities I saw, and the appreciation and support from Khalid Bhai gave me the confidence that I will be able to manage the several simultaneous pressures well and that I was not going to wait for another two years.

Once again, that unbeknownst omnipotent force, which I was still sceptical of and not willing to acknowledge, was at work.

In far off Tirur, a small but historical town in Malappuram district of Kerala, my eventual life-partner-to-be was, unawares, slowly progressing towards our eventual tryst.

Girija was born in Mahé on 12 August 1968, the youngest of three daughters of Vellora Madathil Kammara Poduval and Palat Kannankai Savithri Amma.

As with the many similarities in our lives, Girija's Achan and Amma were a study in contrast.

Achan, a retired army man, was a very physically fit, hardworking, strict, commanding figure who could never sit still and who brooked no dissent.

His wishes and commands were the unwritten writs that ruled the house and its four other occupants.

Achan was from a place called Karamel, a few miles north of Payyannur and Mahadevagramam. He is from the Poduval sect, originally part of the Nair community. Poduval, meaning general administrator, is a title given by the temple because the people of that particular group were given the duty of looking after the vast properties of the temples.[6]

(Hence the Poduvals from Thrissur and its surroundings, who are entrusted with the work inside the temple, are different.)

Achan was the nephew of late V.M. Chinda Poduval, who belonged to the Vellora family. This family held extensive landed properties in the region from Annur (south) to Vellore (north).

This uncle was an uncrowned king of the area—very aristocratic and affluent. Despite such circumstances, there was an insistence to study *jyothisham* and astrology as prevalent in Payyanur in those days. Achan did not accede, and because he had an inclination to join the army, he persisted and got his way.

By the time he had returned from the army, he was an excellent radio/wireless engineer. He was a much sought-after person in

---

6   Poduval is part of the Ambalavasi (temple-dwelling) community. They were considered to be temple caretakers. See Wikipedia: The Free Encyclopedia. 'Ambalavasi.' Available at https://en.wikipedia. org/wiki/Ambalavasi.

the cinema and theatre circles as a sound engineer and would travel extensively in the northern parts of Kerala to repair the sound systems in theatres.

Amma belonged to the Adiyodi sect, a class of Nairs. Amma's father was from Thazhekkattu Mana; he owned extensive landed properties from Trikaripur to Nileshwar. Amma lost her father when she was three years old.

After the death of her father, the family shifted to Vellachal in Kodakkad village, now in Kasargod district. In those days, the girls were not allowed to get a school education. Instead, they were taught at home by appointed teachers. Hence, she was proficient in Hindu scriptures even though she was not formally educated in a school. Her grandfather (mother's father) Thazhekkattu Manayil Cheria Krishnan Thirumumpu was responsible for her basic education.

Amma was a demure, quiet homemaker, always behind the scenes, making sure that the curt, brusque and very strict disciplinarian Achan's wants were met very punctually, lest he throw one of his tantrums which would spoil the day for all of them.

CHAPTER TWENTY

Girija Reminisces

GIRIJA HAS BEEN A great partner and support throughout all these years, right from when we shared an apartment with friends in the thronging, crowded areas of Deira, Dubai, all the way to our own sprawling five-bedroom villa, which we share with our three sons, in the heart of Dubai. It is in the midst of the beautiful setting of Sobha Hartland, part of the Mohammed Bin Rashid Al Maktoum City master development.

So when I started writing this book, I requested her to pen down her thoughts and recollections of her very early past, about which, I must admit, I have not too much insight.

As is her nature, she readily agreed to capture her past, right from the beginning. And this is how she narrated it:

I was born in Mahé, a small historical town, also known popularly in Malayalam as Mayyazhi. It is now a municipality in Mahé district, one of the four districts of the Union Territory of

Puducherry (also known as Pondicherry), which was earlier part of French India.

My family happened to reach Mahé because my father started a small-scale unit to manufacture transformers.

Achan first set up a radio repair shop and then expanded to a small factory making radio transformers. Very disciplined and hardworking by nature, he never sat still for a second, always toiling.

Since the unit was situated in Mahé, he aptly named it the French India Electronic Corporation (FIECOR). For this, he got all the support from the great Poomully Raman Namboodiripad. I have faint memories of having visited the famous Mana with my father. His daughter Rema used to take me and my sister inside while father had discussions with Raman Namboodiripad. Due to trade union problems, he was forced to shift the unit to Tirur in Malappuram district, where setting up an industry was encouraged through sops like tax exemptions.

Unlike Mahé, Tirur was considered an industrially backward area and it was easier to get government subsidies to start small-scale industries.

Though I lived for the first four years of my life in Mahé, which is situated at the mouth of the Mahé River (in Malayalam called Mayyazhi Puzha) and is surrounded by the state of Kerala with Kannur district enveloping the union territory on three sides and Kozhikode district forming the other border, my earliest memories are from Tirur.

Mayyazhi and Mayyazhi Puzha (Mahé and Mahé River) have been part of Kerala's cultural and literary lore since the publication of *Mayyazhippuzhayude Theerangalil* (in Malayalam meaning 'On the Banks of the River Mayyazhi'), a Malayalam language novel by M. Mukundan.

This 304-page tome, first published in Malayalam in 1974 and widely considered as the author's magnum opus, vividly describes the life, times and scenes capturing the political and social background of Mahé, the former French colony, in a lucid yet allegorical style. It was translated into English in 1999 as *On the Banks of the Mayyazhi* and into French in 2002 as *Sur les rives du fleuve Mahé.* The translations have won international acclaim.

Tirur, a town and municipality in Malappuram district, boasts of the oldest railway station in Kerala and, along with the stations at Tanur, Parappanangadi and Vallikkunnu, is also part of the oldest railway line in the state laid from Tirur to Beypore, which started functioning on 12 March 1861. It was extended from Tirur to Kuttippuram via Tirunavaya in the same year.

The very next year, in 1862, the line was further extended from Kuttippuram to Pattambi and again from Pattambi to Podanur in the same year. The existing line between Chennai and Mangalore was later built as an extension of the Beypore–Podanur line.

Never did we imagine, not in our wildest dreams, that this historic railway line would eventually, much later, disastrously, become part of our lives.

Railway disasters seem to have somehow eerily found their way into the saga of northern Kerala.

Tirur wrote its name indelibly into the history books with the infamous wagon tragedy of 1921, which involved 64 of the 100 rebel prisoners being sent by train from Tirur to the Central Prison, Bellary, Madras Presidency, by the British colonizers, suffocating to death in a closed railway freight car wagon from Tirur to Podanur.

My eldest sister Sreelatha was very studious and as soon as she finished her bachelor's degree, she got a job with Federal Bank. She was much older, with a gap of close to 10 years with Geetha, my second sister. She was first away from home for her work and then because she got married.

As a result of that, I became closer to Geetha, and maybe the small age difference between us helped.

My close and select group of friends were Beena, Leena, Ranjini and Vasantha, who were my soulmates and constant companions on the short walks to school and back.

My lower primary schooling, from the first to fourth class, was completed in Government Lower Primary School, Trikkandiyur, Tirur, between 1973 and 1977.

With that school equipped to teach students only up to Class 4, I had to move to the Aided Upper Primary School in Trikkandiyur, Tirur, a short, leisurely 10-minute walk as with the LPS, to complete studies from the fifth to seventh classes, from 1977 to 1980.

In school I was quite diligent in my studies, and even though not a topper, I fared quite well. I completed Class 8 to 10 at the Government Girls High School, Bettath Pudiyangadi (also known as B P Angadi), about three kilometres from home. My friends and I would take the Kerala State Road Transport Corporation (KSRTC) buses or the many privately run buses from home to school on a 10-paisa ticket (around US$0.012 or 1.2 cents).

Government schools did not have the luxury of owning and operating school buses then. In all the schools that I attended, the medium of instruction was Malayalam.

Having obtained good marks in the Secondary School Leaving Certificate examination, in June 1984, I secured admission in the pre-degree course and opted for the Second Group comprising Physics, Chemistry and Biology, the successful completion of which with high marks would make me eligible to join the MBBS course. I studied at the prestigious and reputed Government College Kasaragod at the capital Kasaragod, which is the northernmost of the 14 districts in Kerala. It is part of the North Malabar region, from where a lot of people have historically sought employment in the GCC countries.

My college was about 215 kilometres and a five-hour train journey away from home, and for the first time in my life, I had to stay in a hostel.

A lot of my relatives studied in Government College Kasaragod. My grandmother also stayed very close to the college. My cousin Usha, now a homeopathic doctor, was my classmate and roommate at the hostel. Every weekend, we would go to our *tharavadu* (ancestral home) to stay with our grandmother.

Achan, with his army training and experience that had made him a very strict disciplinarian, abiding by precise timings and perfect orderliness, had also brought up his three daughters to be self-reliant, independent and hardworking.

Very matter-of-fact in all dealings and interactions, he would sometimes put off even close neighbours, relatives and friends by cutting short small talk and walking away from them in the middle of a conversation, abruptly excusing himself to attend to his work.

With that reputation, we did not have too many friends, relatives and neighbours exchanging pleasantries or gossip or even local rumours.

Our family was quite insular, cut off from the community, the exact opposite of Raju's family's close interaction with friends, relatives and neighbours.

But after one year away from home, I started feeling very homesick and badly wanted to stay with my Amma.

So for the second year of the two-year pre-degree course, because of the longing to be near home and visit parents more frequently, it was decided that I would transfer to Farook College, Feroke, Kozhikode district—a beautiful, well-equipped college campus set in a luxuriant sylvan environment with a vibrant atmosphere. I was thrilled to be able to go home to Tirur every weekend.

Again, with commute from home in Tirur to the college in Feroke involving a 90-minute journey, about an hour by train from Tirur to Kozhikode and then a 30-minute bus ride onward to Feroke, it was decided that I would stay in a hostel.

I would have continued to remain a diligent but average student, but a couple of events in my life changed that and made me extremely determined to be numero uno in whatever I do.

With not enough marks to gain entry to a medical college, and not being particularly enamoured by science after studying it for two years, I chose to study B.Com and joined one of the best colleges offering that course in the area—Pocker Sahib Memorial Orphanage College (PSMO) in Tirurangadi town, Malappuram district, a government-aided private junior college affiliated to the University of Calicut.

Although it was initially a government-aided junior college affiliated to the University of Kerala when it was established in 1968, after the reorganization of universities in Kerala state, it was re-affiliated to the University of Calicut.

For someone with a science background and that too from a different college, adjusting to the institution and new commerce subjects took a while.

And in that transitioning phase, I faced one of the worst insulting, humiliating moments of my life.

I was quite excited to leave hostel life and science behind, preferring to become a day scholar even though the one-way trip to college took almost 30 minutes. I was also excited to study new subjects that were closer to earthly matters. With a firm eye on getting a job as quickly as possible to support my parents and family, I also surmised that a degree in commerce would help in opening up new job prospects.

So it was with great excitement that I entered the accountancy class being conducted by a very reputed professor who was also the head of Department of Commerce.

The professor had a different method of exercising control over the students, with his harsh and sarcastic remarks. I always became his prey, because I had no commerce background. No wonder I felt humiliated.

The humiliation acted like a wake-up call. I decided to outwit the teacher by concentrating fully on studying the subject. Finally, I could become the college topper. I had also outshone the class in the professor's subject with a creditable 92 per cent score. I must thank the professor who was instrumental in inspiring me to achieve the level that I am at now. The professor's method was bitter, but the outcome was sweet.

My all-time high marks held good for four to five years as the college record and only then was it broken.

And moreover, I felt a quiet thrill when he asked me to stay on for M.Com and get the first rank in the university.

Retribution, M.Com and the rank were never in my mind. Joining the Chartered Accountancy course and getting a job was the only priority.

By then, three years of exposure to commerce studies had instilled in me a deep love for all the allied subjects, and without any career guidance or counselling, I had gathered that I would get a remunerative job after the prized Chartered Accountancy course. Once again, I decided to pursue that dream with all the energy and grit that I had.

Having qualified through the direct entry route stipulated by the ICAI, by virtue of obtaining more than 50 per cent marks in the B.Com course, my next step was to enrol with the ICAI for the CA intermediate course.

After doing all that was required, as prescribed, I had to register for practical training for three years—a span referred to as articleship in the industry.

For that, I had to find a reputed firm nearby so that I could commute from home and avoid the expenses associated with staying away. And I wanted to be with Amma as much as I could.

With quick research I found the firm Varier & Associates.

As luck would have it, Achan knew the Tirur branch partner of the firm, who was the son of his very close friend and our neighbour, Advocate Vijaya Raghava Varier. So Achan approached him first, and he in turn suggested that I work in the Kottakkal branch.

That firm was also Kottakkal Arya Vaidya Sala's auditor and their office was located very close to home in the Ashraf Building, Town Hall Road, Thazhepalam, Tirur. The firm was known for providing the right environment and training opportunities to articles under its branch partner CA Mohan Das Varier, and I registered under him.

They also had a branch in nearby Kottakkal under branch partner CA Bhaskara Varier, and I had the privilege of working with one of the biggest clients, the world-renowned Kottakkal Arya Vaidya Sala, famous around the globe for its heritage and expertise in the Indian traditional medicine system of Ayurveda.

With steely determination to complete the course and get a job as quick as possible, I put in much more effort than required and passed both groups of the intermediate examination at the first available opportunity with very good scores and duly registered myself for the CA final course, continuing my articleship in the same firm.

From the very experienced branch partners, my colleagues and close friends Balakrishnan, Prakash, Anil and Suresh at Varier & Associates, I learned that the final exam was a very tough one and needed a lot of preparation.

After checking around I found that institutes in Madras offered the best training courses.

There were a wide variety of institutes there, and they all offered intensive and focused training. The students from there had very high success rates.

I vetted all such training academies and found that private-run ones were very expensive—I just could not afford them—and that the one run directly by the ICAI at their Southern India Regional Council office in ICAI Bhawan, Nungambakkam, Madras, where they charged very reasonable fees, was among the best.

It was a very easy decision to make.

That meant that for the first time in my life, I had to live alone for an extended period outside Kerala, about 650 kilometres away from home, reaching which by train took almost 12 hours.

Toughened by the training at home and life experiences and hell-bent on getting my CA and thereafter a well-paying job, I was ready.

I sought Achan and Amma's blessings.

Having moulded all his daughters into three very confident, independent and strong-willed women, Achan had no hesitancy in giving his assent and promptly slid under the hood of the car to tinker with some minor repair work.

But Amma, as much as she wanted me to chase my dreams and invoked all the Gods she knew for their abundant protection and benediction for her youngest daughter, was sad to see me go as she waved me goodbye.

Once again, I set out on my own, like many times before, to Madras, a completely strange land, taking my first overnight train alone, with just the telephone number and address of a relative.

Reaching the hot and sultry historical city, I took an auto to my relative's house and had a bit of a rest. And then joined the academy.

The ICAI conducts exams every six months, in May and November. The preparatory classes are conducted for five months prior to each session. It is not a regular class, like at university, but involves much more of self-study, guided by experienced professionals.

Unlike with formal studies in colleges and universities, the batches are not a fixed set of students attending classes for a set term or period. There are students from all over India, mostly from the southern states, participating randomly to suit their convenience, usually in line with their tentative exam schedules.

I attended four batches during and after the articleship, prior to the intermediate Group I and Group II, and then final Group I and Group II exams.

Achan would send me ₹1000 every month to cover my expenses. Every time I received that money, I would dread accepting and using it, ashamed that even at the age of 23 I was still depending on the scant resources of my father. Caught in a bind, aggrieved at my inability to fend for myself, I did the only thing I could do—concentrated solely on my studies.

Just studies, nothing else. No outings, no leisure, no friends. Straight from the hostel to the institute and back. Even after many months of stay in that metropolis, I was a complete stranger to the city.

I did very well in the first group of the CA final exams.

The next one I did in the November of 1992 was not that easy.

I was apprehensive. Would I pass or would I have to appear again? Would I qualify or, like many I knew, spend several years trying to clear the papers to make the grade as a CA?

That would have meant I had to spend more of Achan's hard-earned money. That I was not willing to accept anymore. No way. I was also getting old. It was getting scary.

For the first time in my life, I was frightened and feeling panicky. The toughness of the November exams deflated my verve and confidence.

I was well into two-and-a-half years of Madras life.

That harbour city was to be my last port of call, before adding the coveted degree to my curriculum vitae and heading for the next destination: a secure, well-paying job.

The time allotted for that process, as per my chart sheet, was draining fast.

The November exam had drained my confidence and shaken me out of complacence. I was now confused and confounded.

It was then that I was told of a marriage proposal, my first.

Achan and Amma were quite old and wanted to see me getting married while they were still healthy and capable of conducting the related functions in the best possible manner.

Being extra sensitive and empathetic, especially in matters concerning my parents, I was also beginning to think about marriage.

CHAPTER TWENTY-ONE

A Marriage Made in Two Matrimonial Columns

BROUGHT UP IN A very strict environment with not much social interaction with other men, I also agreed to what is known as an 'arranged marriage', when parents would, after an often-rigorous process of evaluating many critical factors, especially the compatibility of the two families coming together via the matrimony, pick the most eligible suitor and family for their kids.

As was customary in those days, one of the ways parents would find suitable partners for their children would be by putting out small advertisements about the kids—a short note with age, qualifications, employment details, caste/religion, physical stature and such—in the classified sections in dedicated matrimonial pages of reputed and popular newspapers and magazines.

We had placed one such ad in *Mathrubhumi Azhchapathippu.*

And from the same publication we learnt about a very qualified person, working in Dubai and on a short leave in Kerala, who was looking for a girl with a qualification in commerce and willing to move to Dubai.

He was a CA and also had an M.Com and an LLB.

He fulfilled one of the most important qualifications that I wanted in my future husband—that he should be equally or more qualified than me. My second requirement was that he should be very hardworking like my role model, Achan.

If he had managed to ace his final CA exam in one go, I knew that he was very smart. That he got his LLB also while doing his CA convinced me he was very, very hardworking, too.

I liked what I saw, at least on paper—literally and figuratively.

And I agreed to see this CA.

He was the first 'boy' I was seeing. I learned later that for him, too, I was the first 'girl'. The parents arranged a convenient date and time for us to meet. He came home on 19 November 1992.

At first sight, I liked him. He was smart-looking, lean, of average height, with his smart cut shirt tucked into well-tailored trousers, which stylishly went all the way down to the heels of the shoes, with the upper edge of the heels just about visible.

He told me later that he liked my dress, too.

I was in a *mundum neriyathum*, a traditional dress worn by women in Kerala, especially for special occasions and festive celebrations. I was wearing a very conservative version of this attire, which is very similar to the iconic Indian sari.

Unlike today, when couples are engaged in a long courtship lasting weeks and months to get to know each other before the marriage, we just had a 15–20-minute-long chat to know a little more than that we already knew through the matrimonial ad and communications between families.

Moreover, he was on a short visit on his annual vacation and was keen on finding a partner on this visit.

He explained about his family, what he wanted to do to support the parents, family, his unmarried younger sister, etc.

I explained a bit about my CA studies and wanted to know more about his job in Dubai.

He went to great lengths to convince me that he had a good job with a CA firm where he held the position of an Audit Manager. I was impressed with that and surmised that with his exceptional education and impressive designation, he must be earning a very good salary, although I did not try to ask about it.

I was fine with the match. He was very qualified, hardworking and had a good job in Dubai, which meant I could also move there, get a good job and make money quickly.

As far I was concerned, all the boxes were ticked.

As always, the most important factor for me would be Achan's views.

He was fine with the boy. He said he liked his polite nature and appreciated his qualifications.

Amma, as usual, acquiesced. When Achan had made up his mind and I had concurred, Amma, as was her role, quietly agreed.

The boy's side, too, said they were happy to proceed.

Since the boy had come on a short leave, both families agreed to forgo some of the pre-wedding events, and instead, decided to have just the wedding.

On 13 December 1992, we were married at Pookayil, Tirur, Malappuram.

CHAPTER TWENTY-TWO

Together
Sharing a Life and Apartment

OURS HAD BEEN A typical Gulfee wedding.

The prospective bridegroom-to-be, the protagonist popularly referred to in Kerala as 'boy' in English and *cherukkan* in Malayalam, goes on a month-long annual holiday in search of the counterpart, called 'girl' and *pennu*, hoping that the long and arduous process can be completed within the month in the first visit itself.

In my case, it was very beautifully orchestrated and well accomplished in the allotted time.

Most importantly, I had found a very beautiful girl of my liking. She also shared my passion for taking care of parents, family and relatives, and thankfully also had the same professional interests.

On the Christmas Day of 1992, I had to temporarily part with Girija.

It was a bit of a heartbreak when I left my wife behind after a short honeymoon period and flew back to Dubai, but I pacified myself with the knowledge that she would be joining me soon.

On my return, I saw that the apartment had been spruced up by my fellow residents, and we had a celebratory party that night.

By this time, the couple in the house, Salu and Jessy, had moved out and there was enough space for a new couple.

With just nine months of employment completed in Dubai and with most of the earnings sent home to take care of parents and family, I did not have a lot of savings and could not afford to move into a house of my own. We would have to continue in that shared accommodation for some more time.

I had alerted Girija about all this during our meeting prior to the wedding when we saw each other for the first time and exchanged notes about ourselves.

Being the understanding, empathetic and caring person that she is, she nodded in percipience. I was relieved.

After a three-month interlude, she flew out to Dubai.

In March 1993, Girija joined us as the newest apartment mate at the Lootah Building, Yusuf Baker Road.

Understandably, she was quite nervous.

Having been brought up in conservative household with stringent rules, regulations and curfews laid down by a father who was a martinet and wanted life to be like a well-practised drill at his command, Girija was quiet and introvertish.

According to the rules of their house, the three sisters were not supposed to spend time unnecessarily with friends, and interactions with male friends were to be at a minimum.

So when Girija came to our house, she was shy and withdrawn, but my extremely understanding and generous friends went out of their way to make her feel at home.

As was to be expected, the ice-breaking took a few days.

But it was inevitable that, cajoled by the mates, she would also join in the daily chores of the house and the mirthful and joyous life we led in that apartment.

Soon, Girija would also take charge of the kitchen with all the inmates contributing generously, each handling specific tasks according to their expertise.

But after a short stint of three months, she went back to Kerala to complete her CA exams.

By the end of 1993, she returned to Dubai.

Trained by her father to handle all sorts of work and never one to sit still, Girija decided to take up a job.

Armed with a CA qualification and a B.Com degree, she worked at several jobs over the years, one of which was coincidentally in JAFZ, which later turned out to be a big blessing, a munificent provider of business for my company.

CHAPTER TWENTY-THREE

Driving Off to a New Beginning

A FEW MONTHS INTO 1994, with a second income coming in and with an intense desire for privacy and togetherness, we decided to rent a house of our own.

With businesses on turbo-charge mode in Dubai and across the UAE, more and more expatriates were coming in to make the most of the boom. Hence real estate prices were quite competitive, more so in Dubai and Abu Dhabi.

But even then, the neighbouring emirate of Sharjah still offered very good housing at relatively affordable prices.

After a bit of deliberation and study, we decided to move to Sharjah.

Once a person regularizes their visa status, one of the first things they seek is a driving licence.

With only a very basic public transport system in Dubai which did not ply with the frequency desired by working people and the connectivity also being very restricted, it was essential to have a driving licence.

Each emirate in the UAE has its own systems and procedures, but a single driving licence is valid throughout the nation.

My work included a lot of client meetings at their offices, which meant that I needed to get a licence and vehicle at the earliest to ease mobility and avoid the dependence on taxis, which were often very difficult to get because of the demand.

The intention of moving to a new home in Sharjah gave it an additional impetus. On 31 August 1993, I obtained my first driving licence. Immediately after that, for the first time in my life, at the age of 31, I bought my own car. I am obsessed with the best and spare no expense required to achieve that.

So, no second-hand car would do for me. I bought a brand new, charcoal grey Mitsubishi Lancer.

After a long wait, that car turned out to be a lance for me, much like the long weapon with a pointed steel head mounted on a wooden shaft, historically used by horsemen while charging the rival army.

Soon, I was shuttling around Dubai, in quest of business, and between office and home in Sharjah, in search of much needed privacy and peaceful times with my wife.

We enjoyed the time in Sharjah, but the travelling was taking its toll on both Girija and me.

For her, the commute from home to office would take a long time, with the traffic on the stretch of road from Sharjah to Dubai being very slow and vehicles lined bumper to bumper.

In a few months, we decided that enough was enough, as the very purpose that had prompted our move—spending quality time together—was not being achieved. We decided to move back to Dubai, although to a much smaller and less convenient apartment in Deira. In August 1994, we moved lock, stock and barrel, vowing never ever to move out of Dubai, come what may.

That apartment, situated just behind the very famous Al Futtaim Mosque on Naif Road, Deira, was home to us till the last quarter of 1995.

For Girija, the commute to work had become significantly shorter. For me, it took less than 10 minutes.

Now we had a lot of time for each other and many more hours for constructive work, as I was really getting into the thick of action and needed all the time I could get.

As it turned out, the following year, 1995, was quite an eventful one.

In early April, I had moved on from my first employer to get the maiden opportunity to set up and drive a business, with a significant profit share, too.

By now I was very familiar with the business landscape and dynamics of Dubai and the UAE and had begun to see the opportunities and was formulating strategies to capitalize on them.

Therefore, 1996 saw the creation of the Certain Audit Bureau, and with the ambition of acquiring upscale clientele, I decided to get a few upgrades.

In the second half of the year, we got an amazing, delightful news—that our first baby was on the way.

Now, for a combination of personal and professional requirements, I could not stay on in the cramped apartment we were in.

My residence had to have a highly reputed address to match the new business circles I was moving in and also to welcome the new arrival to the family.

At that time, Al Riqqa was a happening place, so we moved there into the Abdul Aziz Al Majid Building.

It was coincidental that my close friend from Kasaragod, Mahmood Bangara, also a CA, lived in that building. He is the son of late Mr B.M. Abdul Rahiman, the Muslim League MLA from Kasaragod in the fifth Kerala Legislative Assembly.

Mahmood is currently into business and has five grown-up children. We still remain good friends.

As is one of my commandments, probably the eighth: Always think big, do big, execute big; never hesitate to spend money, get the best appurtenances. I thought it was time to follow this commandment and get a new car.

The best vehicle that I could afford that time was that superb German combination of style, design and engineering, the product aptly described by the company as Best or Nothing.

Or, as they say in German, *Das Beste Oder Nichts*.

I also firmly believe that for me it has to be the best or nothing. I wanted the best.

I drove a spanking new Mercedes-Benz out of the showroom.

CHAPTER TWENTY-FOUR

A Star Is Born, and then Two Follow

LIFE HAD NOW SETTLED into a clockwork routine.

I was pushing myself very hard at work, simultaneously developing new businesses, servicing existing clients and maximizing opportunities with existing clients and the already established network.

Girija, as usual, was helping me with my work, but more importantly, eagerly waiting for the baby's arrival.

A lot of women prefer to go back to the comfort of their parents' home for the required pre- and post-natal care. Expatriate wives often miss the intimacy of a large family around them during the pregnancy period.

Girija too preferred to be at home with her parents and flew back to Kerala.

On 22 June 1997, much to the family's delight, our first born arrived in our midst at Surya Hospital, Tirur. Girija's parents, who had rightly been pampering her all the while, were there with her.

My Achan and Amma were thrilled too and visited the mother and baby. Achan named him Aravind, as suggested by me. We all loved the name and made it official. Our very busy life was getting even busier.

With the business stabilizing and moving into higher gear, we discussed and decided that it was better for Girija to give up her job in JAFZ and join Certain Audit Bureau, which by now had moved to the Gargash Centre.

In 1998, my life partner also became my business partner.

She was by now a super contributor, taking care of the baby, managing the chores of the house and putting in long hours of work.

With the turn of the new millennium, we moved to a more elegant and plush office space in Gulf Towers, Oud Metha.

Along with that move, we also decided to shift residences.

And there were a couple of very compelling reasons prompting that decision.

In late 1999, we found that little Aravind was to get a companion. The new arrival was to join us around late 2000.

With the new workspace being in a peaceful, quiet neighbourhood, a move to a residence around there would reduce the commute time significantly and also make it easier for Girija to tend to Aravind and also the new baby.

Luckily for us, we found a very spacious, newly constructed, well-appointed two-bedroom apartment just next to the office building and that, too, on top of a shopping centre with a supermarket.

That one move would prove to be a time saver.

Once again, Girija flew back to Kerala and was happy to join her parents, who again coddled her and also took loving care of a very naughty Aravind who, with his boundless energy, had started skittering all over the place.

Our second baby joined us on 16 September 2000, again in Surya Hospital, Tirur.

This time, the naming right was taken by my wife's uncle, P.K. Kunjikrishnan Adiyodi, who named him after my Achan upon our suggestion: Madhav Menon.

With the business booming, family blooming and having moved to a spacious house, I thought it was also time to trade the compact German car for a safer, roomier, sporty utility vehicle.

For that what better than the Toyota Land Cruiser. As the tagline said, 'Toyota. Everyday.' For me it was, for the next two years.

Then I would opt for more Kings of the Road.

The best among them is my Yellow Hummer H2, which I bought in 2002. By then, we were also expecting our third baby.

Sadly, this time Girija would not be able to go home and be with Amma, who had already left us tragically.

She did not want to go home, where without Amma's loving and caring touch, Achan would have found it very difficult to manage two young, sprightly tots and also her pre- and postnatal needs.

Fortunately, my Achan and Amma joined us in Dubai to provide all the familial love and care that Girija required for her third delivery, which was very close to the first anniversary of Amma's passing.

On 18 June 2002, our third prince joined us.

Girija and I were thrilled.

Govind Menon would complete our family.

We consider ourselves very lucky that both our parents could visit us and stay with us for extended periods.

In 1998, my Achan and Amma first visited us and since then have come over many times and once stayed with us for over two years at a stretch.

More reluctant to travel abroad, Girija's Amma visited us in early 2000 and father stayed with us in 2004. Very disappointingly for all of us, they could do that only once each.

We enjoyed their visits, especially the kids and their grandparents, who revelled in each other's company.

For me it was a great pleasure and privilege to treat Achan and Amma, who were used to a very tough and simple living, to some of the finer things in life—the best that money could buy.

I could often see the uncontrollable pride and unrestrained gratification in Achan. Though he was reserved and not too expressive, his actions would give away his inner feelings.

The way he took pride in wearing a suit and tie, how he loved to sit on my swivel chair and spin on it, how much he enjoyed the long drives in my cars—all this would fill me with enormous pride.

In just 10 years we had come a long way. A very long way.

Starting out with nothing but each other and a whole lot of dreams, Girija and I had traversed quite far, from a sharing accommodation with friends to our own nest with three wonderful babies, a fast-expanding business and a Midas touch turning all our ventures into gold, partly due to luck and timing and mostly due to our hard work.

Both of us considered ourselves blessed for we could provide for and take care of our families in ways we had never imagined possible when we began our journey on 13 December 1992.

Many the world over are fearful of the number 13.

Triskaidekaphobia is not for us.

We actually believe that the number means special blessing. That's exactly what our lives turned out to be.

CHAPTER TWENTY-FIVE

Employee Turns Entrepreneur

IN THE SECOND QUARTER of 1999, I applied to the UAE Ministry of Economy, and on 5 May in the same year, I got the licence to practice auditing as a profession.

With the new licence, as I had been dreaming for a long time, I changed the name of the company from what I thought was a very unprofessional name, more apt for an advertising agency—Certain Audit Bureau—to one which had a historic name, like some of the revered institutions that had just the surname of the partner/s as the moniker: Menon & Associates.

Under the guidelines of the Ministry of Economy, the regulatory body in the country for the accounting profession, a practicing CA cannot hold a partnership in another firm.

So that precluded the boss having a role in the new company and its structure.

The new local partner of the current venture was to be, again, Ms Safiya Haji Akbar Mohammed, the Emirati backer of the erstwhile Certain Audit Bureau.

I also changed the status of my employment visa. I moved from Mak & Partners on to my own Menon & Associates visa, gave up the signing authority and parted ways with my boss and the company that had given me a haven, a breakthrough, a toehold and a lifeline when I had landed in Dubai, armed with a coveted qualification, a great CV, several dreams and not much else.

The parallel college student from Cheekilode was starting a venture with his own name on the company plaque, prominently displayed outside the new office, reading 'Menon & Associates'.

CA Raju Menon was the Managing Partner.

Expanding the business profitably was consuming me. I recruited new people. We were growing considerably.

Most of our major projects were related to consulting and particularly company setup. It was also a very remunerative business in those days because it did not require too many people to service it. The overheads were low and the margins were high.

By then two very dynamic people had joined us—Pushpan in company setup and Harminder Singh focusing solely on audit work. It was a synergistic combination and in less than two years at the Gargash Centre, we quickly grew from around five to over 20.

Change was the only constant. And hard work too.

With the success provided by an expanding, driven team working very hard, we had to move again.

The new millennium was upon us. We had to be Y2K ready.

CHAPTER TWENTY-SIX

The Ordinary Concrete House Turns into a Villa

FOR THE MILLIONS OF expatriates in Dubai, the UAE, the GCC and the world over, one of the first investments after starting to earn is purchasing a new house, building a home or refurbishing an existing one.

In Cheekilode we had a basic house, for which, much against our wishes, we could not even make a provision for a garage because we were then too consumed by fears of what our family, friends and neighbours would think of our audacity and opulence—if a car shed could be considered as one.

So at that time, being worried about small village chatter and ridicule, we had quietly shelved the dream of having a car shed.

But now it was time to stand tall and fulfil the dreams that we had then by giving them a concrete structure.

It was not to be just another house.

By 1994, I had started the reconstruction and development of the house, building many extensions.

One of the first additions was a garage into which a brand-new Ambassador, the packhorse of Indian roads then, seemingly with the ability to carry unlimited passengers and limitless cargo in its cavernous boot, was driven in and parked, smelling of all the newness of a vehicle off the showroom.

In 1999, that basic home was to be transformed into a spacious villa, with luxurious fittings and furnishings to enhance comfort and car garages that could house a couple of automobiles.

My elder brother Unnikrishnan, who had been teaching at the nearby Kolathur Aided Upper Primary School for decades, his wife Soumini, also a teacher at the Aided Upper Primary School, Cheekilode, very close to home, and their children have been living there ever since.

Both are retired now.

Their daughter Shalini is a doctor and son Vishnu is a CA—following his uncle's footsteps to become only the second CA from Cheekilode in 33 years.

With Chettan and family comfortably settled in, it was time to create my own nest.

And I would spin off from that ancestral home.

By the power of that divine force, that grace, I would beaver away, accumulating fortunes for the present and future generations that my ancestors, parents and I had not even dreamt of in those early days in Cheekilode.

CHAPTER TWENTY-SEVEN

New Millennium, New Beginnings, Million Vistas

WE WELCOMED THE YEAR 2000 and the millennium with the rest of the world, with hope, anxiety, trepidation and apprehension.

On the family front, Girija and I were eagerly waiting to welcome our second child. But the overwhelming emotion was unbridled optimism.

The world had successfully survived the Y2K scare and I felt that positive energy, right at the beginning of the year, fire us all up.

We were experiencing significant growth.

At work, one of the concerns coming up in team meetings and from the experience of the staff concerned with business development was that the growth of Menon & Associates was being restricted by the stand-alone nature of the firm and its lack of an international affiliation through a network or association of consultants.

With the UAE not having an overseeing, regulatory body for chartered accountants, like the ICAI in India, it was felt that to garner business from clients such as banks and multinational corporations, it was imperative to obtain a valuable partnership with a reputed global association who, within their network, had renowned independent accounting, audit, tax, legal, advisory, financial, immigration and technology services firms across the world.

This was the same concern and feedback that the Indian CA qualification was not adequate for the cosmopolitan clientele of Dubai and the rest of the UAE and that they were comfortable with those who held US or UK qualifications, which inspired me to get the very valued and prestigious American accounting qualification—Certified Public Accountant, or CPA.

Over the years, with Indian CAs having proved their mettle across many verticals in some of the best multinational and national firms based in the UAE, it has come to be accepted as one of the best qualifications in the field.

I am proud that our organization has also contributed significantly to raising the profile of Indian CAs in the UAE.

At Menon & Associates, we shortlisted a few international partners who were an ideal fit for us, initiated communication with them and found that at that point, the association that complemented us best and would give us the best impetus was Morison International (later, in 2016, two successful, well-established organizations, Morison International and KS International, merged to form Morison KSi).

Like the rest of the world, we were also cutting loose some of the ropes that were tying us down.

We started the new year and millennium on a triumphant note.

We had transformed from being a stand-alone accounting and consulting firm to becoming part of a multinational association.

Morison Menon was the name of the new entity, with partner firms across the world. Hearing about our rapid growth, expansion and highly ethical work approach, a CA with an existing portfolio of business approached me with a proposal to start a branch in Sharjah in partnership.

I had a meeting with Saju Augustine, then working with a well-known CA firm, was impressed with his acumen, vision and passion and knew he would fit in comfortably with the organization. I decided to go ahead with the partnership.

In 2000, Morison Menon, Sharjah, became the first branch of the firm.

In parallel, we also moved from the Gargash Centre in bustling Deira to the shiny aluminium-and-glass building with a unique curtain wall design—Gulf Tower—newly completed in 2000 in the quiet and serene surroundings of Umm Hurair, Oud Metha. We rented a 2,500 square feet office space.

The shiny new signage on the building read Morison Menon.

With the new global affiliation, travel to the various business hotspots around the world to attend conferences and meetings became a regular event.

A significant part of our international travel involved accompanying the UAE delegations to global events and exhibitions to promote the country as an investment destination.

Over these years, such trips and holidays have taken me to almost all continents and over 40 countries.

CHAPTER TWENTY-EIGHT

Growth Strategy

I HAD LEARNED A LOT from my time in Dubai.

Four key takeaways that I'd gained as an employee at Mak & Partners and while managing Certain Audit Bureau, Menon & Associates and Morison Menon would help me greatly grow my businesses.

They were: 1) dealing with clients, 2) taking risks, 3) trying out new things, and 4) empowering key staff.

To those four I added two of my own that I would consider a prime necessity in fostering a competitive, loyal, creative, equitable, industrious, assiduous work environment and honest work ethics.

These were: 5) rewarding people appropriately, and 6) never compromising on professional ethics.

Morison Menon was now at a critical threshold.

Business was thriving; we were optimally staffed, had a new prestigious office address and were now part of a reputed global network.

Further growth was possible in two ways—through mergers and acquisitions (M&A) or organic growth.

My sharp financial, accounting and business acumen told me that we were not big enough to take the M&A route and that gradual growth was the way forward.

One of our first test cases was the Jebel Ali branch, which had triggered the quick spurt of growth while we were Certain Audit Bureau and then Menon & Associates.

To capitalize on the massive growth that was taking place, I had set up an unmanned office there. My colleague Pushpakaran K. Parambath, popularly known in our offices and in business circles as Pushpan, and I were the drivers of that branch, developing business at a rapid pace and also taking care of the operations through very hard work and long work hours. Our staff based in the main office would provide us with all the back-office support required.

With the introduction of several new commercial laws designed to ease business in the free zones, JAFZA was on an overdrive.

With the benefits drawing global attention, a lot of overseas clients were interested in setting up businesses in JAFZA and other free zones.

Though they were from all across the world, the main interest was from Europe and the Far East and there was a great business opportunity in helping such clients set up their companies in JAFZA.

Morison Menon was among the first consulting firms in the UAE with company setup expertise.

We would advertise heavily in industry trade magazines and the yellow pages and handled the needs of clients with absolute professionalism and cheerful energy, and in turn we started getting a lot of referrals from delighted clients.

With a healthy roster of clients being sourced by us, JAFZA was very pleased with our work and facilitated our business by providing excellent service and quick turnaround times, further enhancing our reputation as a reliable, quick and efficient company-setup services provider.

We put in place a one-window clearance system whereby, after just one visit to us to sign the necessary application forms, documents and allied legal papers, clients could return to their bases and we would diligently carry out the remaining spadework to complete the task.

We would work very closely with JAFZA officials, prepare the company formation documentation, obtain all the necessary approvals, get the visas for the investor(s) and organize any other personal/bespoke requirements for clients and forward the necessary entry permits and clearances so that they could enter the UAE and start their operations, all in quick time.

Pushpan, the team and I worked very hard and it paid off.

We then replicated that expertise across all the new free zones that were springing up.

For many of them, we were the first company setup experts sourcing clients in large numbers.

The success of our first free-zone branch, the one in JAFZA, was quite remarkable. In the first year itself, in 2001, we had made a significant profit.

So we had a licence and office from JAFZA that we ran as a separate profit centre. But for the most part, it was being operated by the support staff initially based at Hor Al Anz and then at the Gargash Centre.

But there was much more business to be generated from that free zone and others that were springing up across the nation.

Harminder Singh, who had joined as an auditor and was promoted to Manager in our audit vertical while at Gargash Centre, had impressed me with his extremely professional, polite demeanour with clients. He was also very committed, was not a clock-watcher and had great communication skills.

To empower him, motivate him further and reward him, I put forth an offer he could not refuse.

Over a coffee I asked Harminder if he would be interested in developing our JAFZA business further, focusing specially on the audit side.

I was prepared to promote him to Partner—by then he was working as Audit Manager—and give him a significant stake in that venture.

Having been in the audit business for a while, it did not take him long to make the calculations and say yes with glee on his face.

On 1 May 2008, the unmanned satellite office became Morison Menon, Jebel Ali. From then it would be steered by Harminder.

That business has been doing very well. The staff strength has grown to around 15, and on our heydays we have an enviable turnover and rake in profits. Later, we added another partner. Yes, as with businesses all over the world, ours were also impacted by the financial crisis of 2008–2009 and then the pandemic in 2020–2021.

But these cycles are an integral part of the business and we have put in place financial buffers to protect us from downside risks.

Once I put my trust and faith in people, which they had earned with their honesty, integrity and commitment, I would empower and incentivize them and give them full freedom to run the business as they wanted. I would never exert any control, maintaining a strict hands-off policy.

However, there are two key functions I keep complete control of to ensure that there is absolute transparency and accountability in the pivotal areas related to the ventures' finances: 1) accounting of company finances and 2) acting as the signatory authority with the financial institutions with which the company deals for all banking needs.

From my experiences, I have learnt that micromanagement of people and businesses is self-defeating. When given the freedom, people bloom.

With experience it became obvious that trusting, empowering and incentivizing people and giving them full freedom to creatively develop the business in their own styles and according to their passion could work wonders.

The last factor—motivating people through financial incentives, abiding by the terms agreed with them and paying their salaries on time—is very important for ensuring that employees are happy and inspired and the work place has a vibrant, positive energy that spurs growth.

If a company breaks such a promise with their staff and does not share what is rightfully due to them, it could lead to significant discontent. This would spread like a nasty cancer, engulfing the whole organization with its negativity.

When such wronged people leave an organization, wounded by the unfair treatment meted out to them, they become ambassadors of hate who will try to tarnish a firm's reputation built over years through the hard work of its diligent, dedicated staff.

Therefore, having grown wise by my experience of many such incidences and having interacted with many who had faced such episodes, I had added one more to the cardinal rules, the seventh: 7) if an employee wishes to leave the organization, part with them on the best of terms, even if they have treated me and the firm unfairly, giving them more than their due, so that they become your goodwill ambassadors.

I strictly abide by all of my commandments, particularly the seventh.

The commandments have always worked for us; the reputation of fairness that we have earned in the market has paid dividends in many ways.

Harminder and Morison Menon's JAFZA office had very successfully proved my theory and provided a template for further branch expansions.

More diligent and dedicated staff and managers would be promoted as partners and new offices would be opened as the firm and its staff all enjoyed growth and therefore accrued personal benefits through enhanced remuneration—increased salaries, bonuses and other pay-outs.

Over the years, a lot of people have asked me how I manage to keep around 15 very senior partners in the organization. Some, like Khalid Al Shams, Harminder, Pushpan, Zeid Qadan, Saju Augustine and, of course, Girija Menon, have been with the organization for a very long time, almost from the very beginning. While some have completed over 10 years with us, others are more recent, around 3–4 years.

I cannot but thank Khalid, who has been with us since our beginning in Hor Al Anz and, as the person in charge of business development and client relations with large corporate houses and local businesses, was instrumental in the company making considerable inroads into the UAE national business segment.

He has been with us since July 1998. He is now the Group's CEO and typifies the dedication and commitment of each and every Kreston Menon employee.

But whether it is a senior who has been with me for long or someone who has joined just a few years back, my operating principles and commandments remain constant and are the guidelines that govern my relationships.

While the seniors have mellowed and settled down into a pattern that every stakeholder is familiar with and knows to play by, some of the younger partners, by the very nature of their age, are naturally more ambitious and aggressive.

Whatever the pressures, I ensure that there is absolute fairness and justice in the business structure being forged and use my tried and tested yardsticks and commandments to maintain consistency in what I do.

May I reiterate that I do not believe accumulating all the wealth for myself. In every partnership, I go out of my way to make sure that the partner is inspired by the equity and benefits on offer.

As an extension of that principle, I proactively, without waiting for the other party to ask, give the best options possible to partners and do not haggle, argue or browbeat them into any contract that they are not comfortable with. As a corollary, neither do I allow them to wrest an unfair bargain from me.

I firmly believe in mutual respect.

Even if they come with proposals that are skewed heavily in their favour, I try to reason with them, show the value they have created riding on the Kreston Menon brand and discuss how much more they can benefit if we work out a mutually agreeable deal.

Often, even the hot-headed young partners, if counselled well and given a data-backed explanation, usually come around to a realistic and remunerative agreement that is beneficial for the firm and for them.

I try, as much as possible, not to let them break away because it is often detrimental to both.

I do not cling on to what belongs to the partner, the share of the value and wealth they created though their intellect, brain and brawn power, for I realize that beyond a point of tolerance, they will break away in frustration and in that process, probably cause harm to both.

My experience has taught me that if we do good work, maintaining the highest standards of sincerity, diligence and ethics and with the larger, best interest of the client as the utmost driver, money will find its way to us. There are no shortcuts for any of the above.

Cut a corner for a quick buck and it could damage both the client and the firm. So that is a strict no-no, and that message is constantly reinforced throughout the organization.

Render unto God the things that are God's, render unto Caesar the things that are Caesar's and render unto the Partner the things that are the Partner's is a commandment I take seriously.

Strictly adhering to the self-imposed guidelines and commandments that are designed to guarantee high levels of ethical behaviour from all stakeholders, especially integrity, honesty, mutual respect, transparency and dignity, we were strengthening our brand.

Towards that end, Sudhir Kumar joined us in 2006 as Partner & Head—Corporate Communications, and further reinforced our marketing and corporate communications capabilities.

I believe in doing things in a big, bold and beautiful manner, never compromising on quality and the quantum required, and Morison Menon was spending nearly AED 1.5 million a year on creating awareness and recall of the brand in all the markets that we operated in through an integrated mix of advertising, public relations and direct marketing.

Some of the main newspapers in the UAE—*Gulf News*, *Khaleej Times*, *The National* and *Gulf Today* are the prominent ones in English—would often quote my views on the industry and allied business developments as a thought leader.

Creating wealth and sharing it with others, which Amma used to do even when she had very little of her own, had subliminally rubbed into my psyche.

And I was revelling in doing what Amma used to do, but this time on a magnificently multiplied scale.

CHAPTER TWENTY-NINE

My (Management) Style

IN ADDITION TO THE personal commandments, I have also over the years developed a unique management style that is derived out of my personal experiences and not academic learning.

My Leadership Style

Being the leader of our organization—which handles 11 major verticals, Audit & Assurance, Bookkeeping & Accounting Services, Payroll Services, Business Advisory & Consulting, IFRS Advisory Services, Company Formation & Corporate Services, Taxation Services, Technology Consulting, Compliance & Anti-Money Laundering, Corporate Governance, Risk, Compliance (GRC) and Corporate Finance Consulting—I have always firmly believed that I should have enough knowledge of every line of business to discuss matters authoritatively, adding value to every interaction and deliberation on related matters with the partners who are driving that segment.

It is also very important to have this insight and knowledge because we deal with clients in over 12 industries—Government & Public Sector, Hospitality, Travel & Transport, Retail, Real Estate & Construction, Manufacturing, Education, Transport & Logistics, Media & Technology, Food & Consumer Goods, Healthcare & Pharmaceuticals, Financial Services, Energy—and as the leader I like to ensure that we are abreast or ahead of the latest trends, patterns and developments in all these areas.

As I have indicated, I abstain from associating with what is not the best or is mediocre.

And I try to motivate all my staff to make sure that they are also passionate about that vision.

Never one to micromanage, I leave the responsibility of powering the business to the partners in charge of those lines. Therefore, I am keen on the big-picture view, not the nitty-gritty. My aim is never to get in-depth knowledge of any sector but my own, because they are not run by me and I do not cramp their styles.

Within the organization, I have CEOs and Partners to run all the 11 verticals, and I make it a point to acquire as much basic knowledge as required of all businesses under our umbrella.

If I get a hunch that the organization is lacking in a particular area and am convinced that a specialist's skill is required to guarantee excellent functioning, I always acquire top-calibre resources with that particular talent.

As much as I am passionate about my company, I also make it a point to be a dispassionate, neutral professional who looks at the business and allied matters objectively.

So I keep a deliberate distance, a very unbiased separation between me the person and my alter ego—the zealous entrepreneur.

This decoupling also inspires me to believe that the organization should not be deprived of its growth if I lack a crucial personal trait that is essential for the firm's progress.

For example, even though I am good at socializing and interacting with prospective clients, I also recognize that sometimes I have my own inhibitions. These may become impediments that work against the interest of the firm, at times leading to the loss of a big deal.

Having realized that, and to offset that negative impact on business, I have acquired employees who are excellent communicators—extroverts who can charm customers into deal-winning delight, thereby bagging lucrative projects despite trying challenges.

I am a life-long learner. I have never stopped studying.

Even the long list of titles after my name—M.Com, LLB, CA, CPA, FAIA—does not really reflect the reading, training and up skilling that I continuously do, always competing with myself and pushing myself to be at par with the latest and even upgrade to the next level.

Every stage of my growth is a deliberate, intentional and planned upgrade.

With the painstaking and intense self-advancement efforts also come magnificent fruits of the labour.

With the wide understanding of a variety of subjects that are relevant to running a business, I am also able to recognize opportunities very fast and take quick decisions.

For example, when someone pitches a new business opportunity to me that might be interesting and within the realm of sectors that I am comfortable with and would like to be involved in, by virtue of my awareness of contemporary business projects, I pick up the intricacies very fast and often in the very first meeting itself tell them if I am interested in furthering our discussions.

I quickly run through the pros and cons in my mind, doing a mental SWOT analysis even while the meeting is still on. If I feel that there is no opportunity in the proposed business, I politely terminate the discussion within 10 minutes and inform upfront that I am not interested. I do not like to waste their time or mine. Once I have made a decision, I stick to it. At least, for the most part.

My Management Style

I give absolute 100 per cent freedom to the heads of the verticals in my organization when they demonstrate the capability and maturity to handle business independently.

My usual assessment and often informal probation time for the boss of a new setup is one year. Within that year, I assess their all-round skills—in handling people, clients, peers, subordinates, seniors, juniors, vendors, subject knowledge, work pressure and so on.

I firmly believe that freedom brings out the creative best in people. I give full operational freedom to get the maximum possible out of the person. This is also a calculated risk because, after thriving on their own, sometimes, some of the division heads tend to believe that the business burgeoned only because of their efforts, conveniently and easily forgetting that the initial support provided from my side in terms of mentoring, brand value, confidence to take risks and such vital factors were critical in fashioning the success.

However, being aware of the high possibility of risk, especially with the younger partners and managers, I have put in place mitigation strategies to counter it.

Such situations can often be managed well by going out of the way to ensure that there is fairness in all dealings. We also clearly, with the help of data and documents, convince the partners and managers why it is so.

Simultaneously, to manage their egos and once again reinforce our equity, I also make it a point to reiterate that they are very valuable assets for the firm, that they are being rewarded suitably and that as the business grows, they will also grow within the organization with suitable promotions and financial benefits.

Sometimes, I even give them economic freedom that goes beyond my share of interest.

One of the remarkable self-imposed strictures that I abide by and am very proud of is not mixing business affairs and my personal propensities and predilections, if any.

Even though mine is a privately owned business, I ensure that the best corporate governance practices prevalent in the most reputed global organizations is the benchmark that we set for ourselves in everything that we do.

Therefore, I deliberately distance myself from the enterprise, considering myself as separate from the organization, so that its independence is safeguarded, and never mix my personal interests and that of the organization, thereby avoiding moral, ethical and operational conflicts that often put partners and staff in awkward situations.

This dispassionate, contemplative delinking has helped me gain the respect of my partners, who also feel emboldened to look at issues with the merit they deserve, without having to worry about my preferences.

That creates a dynamic, bold work culture that shuns internal politics and mediocrity and is truly meritocratic, acknowledging and rewarding genuine, good output.

On occasions, I intentionally play the devil's advocate, stirring debates to reaffirm to the team that I always consider the organization's interest first and my personal interests only thereafter, subliminally also conveying to all staff that, that should be how the firm works.

For a team of around 500 employees across 11 verticals in 9 sectors located in 17 offices to thrive in extremely competitive and fast-moving markets such as the UAE, GCC and India, all members have to pull their weight and do it quickly.

As the captain, I lead by example. I am very quick in decision-making.

Even though I do not interfere, I keep a keen watch on the dashboards of all ventures and am ahead of the happenings, so if the chief of a division seeks an opinion, I come up with it fast enough so that the subsequent actions can be carried out in good time.

Also, as part of my resolve not to mix the business with any other projects and propositions, even if I get a warm, sincere and cordial invitation to join a client's business, I politely decline the offer.

My Character

Affable, amiable and very genteel by nature, I seldom pick fights or engage in verbal duels.

Very rarely, when pushed to the extreme, even if I get into one of those one-in-a-million arguments, I do not have it with people who are less smart and less talented than me. In such situations, I avoid a quarrel, and even if there is some difference of opinion, I support the other person.

If pushed beyond my extremely high tolerance levels, or if challenged and required to pick up a bout against my grain, I will only fight with people who are of much higher calibre than me.

Otherwise, I just walk away from a fight. I am a peace-loving, non-aggressive person.

Amma's Munificence Becomes My Virtue

Having grown up watching Amma and her benevolent ways, they have become an indelible part of me and my character.

I have always believed that people around me should lead content, meaningful lives which in turn make them feel the same way about the people around them.

With that in mind, I constantly try to facilitate their good living.

Over the years, this approach has led me to my own version of personal and corporate social responsibility.

I realized early on that diluting the resources I have allocated for philanthropic efforts by targeting too many causes does not serve any purpose. The resources can be used more effectively to better the lives of family, friends and acquaintances.

To this end, I strongly support my close and distant relatives and also accept them into my organization. I also support my friends who need a helping hand and provide succour to individuals whom I have known over the years and unfortunately have not been able to improve their situations, financially and otherwise.

I get an immense sense of fulfilment and satisfaction when, through my efforts, they are happy.

I am strictly against nepotism, cronyism and favouritism in public life and government affairs in India. But I also think that privately run businesses have the right to do what they deem best, in line with their attitudes, because it is a performance risk that they take with due consideration to the many factors involved.

And obviously for that institution, employing that particular person must be giving the best return on investment, all relevant factors considered.

It is very well established and recognized throughout the organization that only the merit of a person and their work output matter and are rewarded, nothing else. There is no place for politics in our office.

Therefore, I do not worry about taking relatives, friends or acquaintances in my organization as employees because all the team members are confident that I will never promote politics and nepotism.

The moment they start working, I do not distinguish them from my other employees. If they are talented, they are further supported through training, counselling and mentoring. If they so desire, I allow them to move out to another organization at any time.

Over the years, I have witnessed and experienced that getting the first break is the most difficult task. Once a person gets the right break, they establish themselves quickly and move up in life very fast.

For those who do not get the right opportunity, life continues to be a struggle that very often lasts for a long time.

Wiser by having undergone such ordeals, I believe in giving the first break to such people who are known to me or have been referred or recommended even if they may not be up to par in qualifications and skills. I know well that getting an opportunity with a professional setup might otherwise be impossible for them. At the initiation, orientation and initial training phases, they are made aware of the out-of-turn chance given to them and further assured that if they deliver, they can progress rapidly.

As in many competitive sports and games, I have deliberately introduced a system of handicapping while recruiting.

To provide a level playing field for all candidates and yet give people I know—my relatives, friends and other jobseekers who have come as references—a bit of an advantage, I have purposefully given a 20 per cent weightage, a talent-scale markup to enhance the chances of their getting selected.

If they are successful and manage to get in, I make it further easier for them through training, coaching and additional tutoring as required.

Having come from very humble beginnings and aware how well the time that we have can be utilized to better our life situation and simultaneously do good and help people improve theirs, I dislike people who waste their time on pettiness and other such trivial pursuits.

As an extension of that line of thinking, I do not harbour any hatred against people.

When there is a difference of opinion with someone, I argue vehemently and forcefully to convince them of the validity of my position, but in a few minutes that aggression is forgotten and I become the friendly, calm person that I am most of the time.

I never carry any hatred or prejudices in my mind, I do not allow myself to be preoccupied with business matters and I never hold on to any animosity against anyone.

Often, it is small upsets that lead to acrimony, bitterness and souring of relationships.

Hence, I do not allow minor clashes to linger and grow into major ego conflicts.

Even if, in the rarest of cases, a major emotional eruption scars me, I make it a point to get rid of all negative thoughts associated with it. I have trained myself to not harbour the hurt beyond a maximum of six months.

Luckily, such long-lasting, extremely painful episodes have been few. And I hope to keep it that way.

Another trait I dislike is duplicity and hypocrisy. I am very upfront and genuine.

When I do not like something, I do not hide my true feelings in diplomacy.

I sit across the table with the person concerned, discuss my concerns openly and seek an amicable solution. That matter is closed there. It does not occupy any space in my mind anymore.

When, as the result of mutual respect, love and care, people show their affection and concern, I relish it, cherish such moments and feel blessed.

Having experienced both scarcity and opulence, and having seen the transformation from one to the other happen in my life in a very short span of time, I am convinced that it is the good deeds of my parents, especially my mother, which were instrumental in that drastic reversal of my fortunes.

This unanticipated success and wealth have shaped my conviction that good deeds make life meaningful and beautiful. They have made me appreciate that life takes on a new meaning when I see that through my altruistic acts, I can add value and joy to the lives of those around me.

Experiencing genuine affection from someone whose life you have touched is very special.

Pushing the Limits

It follows naturally from my obsession to be the best that I have to give every initiative much more than my best. I push my limits to the maximum possible extent.

To achieve my goal of attaining superlative performance, I have developed a trait that has worked wonders.

Once I set a target, I motivate myself and my team to give it our best. I leave no stones unturned. I stay the course with all I have.

Despite such an effort, if I do not acquire what I set out to, I am at peace knowing that I did my best and consider the case closed.

It is done and dusted.

If required, the team and I perform follow-ups of the task.

Again, if we do not achieve our goal, there are no regrets, no ifs and buts.

The case diary is reviewed once again with the team to see if we gave it our best possible effort and check whether we inadvertently missed out on any key factor. The necessary learnings and shortfalls, if any, are noted.

And the case is closed. We move on.

Some Red Lines

I do not like stasis and inertia in my businesses.

Especially in a very aggressive and dynamic market like Dubai, where there are players at all business levels—from the gilt-edged multinationals of the Big Four, to the next rung of elite networks such as Kreston Menon and, at the other end of the spectrum, the aspiring newbies—constantly striving for a larger share of the market.

To expand in such a market, it is critical that the organization takes calculated financial risks. I do not shy away from that. When required, extremely confident in the abilities of the team, I take bold business decisions that might be vulnerable to monetary perils.

But there is one bigger risk for me and the organization: anathema.

I do not play with our professional honour and standing. We never take risks that will soil our reputation.

If I perceive that there is that possibility in a project, a professional relationship or a deal, I make sure we steer clear of it, however lucrative it might be.

That is a line never to be crossed.

The organization and I make it a point to maintain our high ethical standards at all times.

May I reiterate that maintaining genial, excellent relationships with people is very important for me and I would like to ascertain that it remains that way even when someone leaves the organization.

I believe they should depart with grace, dignity and pride, whether the person is leaving due to underperformance or for better prospects.

As much as I desire a congenial and gregarious atmosphere in the office, I am also a driven taskmaster who politely and professionally seeks the best from the team.

That means that I do not work only for earning respect from the people of my organization. My primary aim is to get things done; winning others' respect is secondary to me.

The bottom line is like this: Let us work hard with a focus to deliver. Then we will share the spoils and celebrate.

Think Big, Do Bigger

I have been very fortunate to have come to Dubai and the UAE and have lived here since 1991.

All the good things in life accrued gradually since then.

My life and lifestyle were transformed to levels unimaginable in my home state and country.

For all that I am eternally thankful to this land and the greatest lesson this city and country taught me: Think Big, Do Bigger.

That is the motto that has driven me ever since and spurs me on even now.

My Ardent Beliefs

The massive metamorphosis of my life, with striking contrasts in every aspect and matrix from the beginning to now, has made me an ardent admirer of the beauty of life and its possibilities.

Amma showed me very early on with her nature and living as an example that life is inherently beautiful and that it is good deeds alone that can make it truly meaningful, enhancing its enchantment even more.

Life has been very kind and generous to me.

I have enjoyed every bit of my life, from childhood until now.

This has been possible only because of the people around me—from my parents, siblings and their families, my beautiful wife and three wonderful children, my in-laws—everyone who has been with me on my journey all the way from that tiny, verdant village in Kerala to the megalopolis that is my workplace and home now.

Now, in turn, I try to spread happiness in the people around me—my immediate family, the extended ménage, the Kreston Menon family and friends from the past and the present.

I am a people's man.

CHAPTER THIRTY

The Consolidation

THE NEW MILLENNIUM HERALDED a lot of changes.

At the beginning of the year, we had shifted to our new office and formalized our agreement with Morison International. Business was on a roll.

At that point we had four offices: the Morison Menon main office in Oud Metha and a branch each in Sharjah, Abu Dhabi and JAFZ.

The business environment was all charged up, the team had fire in the belly and I wanted to consolidate to capitalize on the reputation and advantages we had built up rapidly over a short period.

We had to move quickly and into new territories.

It was not only Dubai and the UAE that were experiencing a new-found energy.

It was being felt across the GCC, and I was on the lookout for geographical expansion into new areas.

I had a significant contact network in, and sound awareness of, the Oman market, having identified talent for that market while at Mak & Partners.

When in 2004 I got the opportunity to start a venture there, I was convinced of the possibilities. In Antony Isaac, I found the right partner who could implement our vision and drive the business.

So the Muscat office became the first international operation of Morison Menon.

While we had very strong audit and company setup units, the diversification of the market in line with the various opportunities mushrooming in the UAE and across the GCC also presented the possibility of a consulting division.

Therefore, in 2004, I also established the Consulting Division.

Initially, I ran it on my own, but later one of our partners was given charge of the division.

In 1999, the year Menon & Associates rebranded, the average closing price of crude oil was US$19.35 after opening at US$12.42 and closing at US$25.76.

By 2004, it had skyrocketed to US$41.51. This was an over 200 per cent increase after opening at US$33.71, hitting a year-high of US$56.37 and closing at US$43.36.

With the global economy firing on all six cylinders and its major engines across the continents guzzling fuel to power its factories, heat and cool its homes and keep its servers up and running, and with planes transporting millions daily across global hotspots and huge container ships ferrying cargo across the far corners, there was an insatiable thirst for energy.

That need for fuel spurred an unprecedented demand, sending oil prices through the roof.

The beginning of 2005 saw even more spectacular figures, with the average closing price of US$56.64 and closing price of US$61.06.

The cumulative impact on the economy and businesses was palpable and throbbing.

The steady increase in prices from 1999 was in parallel with the establishment and growth of our businesses.

To handle the quantum growth, our team was expanding rapidly, too.

We had swelled to around 70 people and, in 2005, we acquired an additional 2,500-square-feet office space adjacent to our office in Gulf Towers, thereby doubling our space.

With the oil and gas sectors witnessing an unprecedented boom, not just the UAE, but all GCC economies benefitted stupendously.

And within the GCC, with their immense oil and gas riches and visionary investments into state-of-the-art technologies for all initiatives from extraction to marketing, including all the various cycles and processes in upstream, midstream and downstream activities, Saudi Arabia, the UAE and Qatar were reaping the benefits and ploughing them back into developing their infrastructures at a furious pace.

In July 2006, the Morison Menon Group secured a licence to operate in the Dubai International Financial Centre (DIFC) as an ancillary service provider. This enabled us to offer bookkeeping and compliance services to existing firms and advisory support to firms looking to register at the DIFC.

By 2007, the average closing price of crude oil had reached US$72.34—an astounding 400 per cent increase compared to the 1999 prices.

We had to move into Qatar, an easily manageable territory.

My flight to Doha was about to land, and the PA announcement asked passengers to refasten their seat belts. For me, this was a clear signal to begin my Doha chapter.

The oil prices were once climbing steeply again, on their way to soaring new highs as we descended on Doha.

Morison Menon Qatar would be captained by me. I was to be ably assisted by my co-partner Kurian Kuriakose, a friend from my CTC Hostel days who still leads the firm successfully.

Meanwhile, in the UAE, drawn by the riches and fame of the gleaming skyscrapers mushrooming across the nation, foreign investors were flocking to the free zones.

With their aggressive marketing, especially in Europe, Africa and Asia, the Ras Al Khaimah Free Zone was attracting a lot of investors, and Saju Augustine, our Sharjah partner, strongly recommended that we also open a branch in Ras Al Khaimah to garner a sizeable share of the company setup business there.

It looked like an extremely promising prospect, and on 13 August 2014, we set up a branch in Ras Al Khaimah with Saju driving the business there.

The oil prices showed no signs of stalling. 2007 closed at US$95.95, and 2008 opened at US$99.67.

But, unbeknown to the world, a lot of mortgage loan offerings, and their bundling into further complicated products known as Mortgage-Backed Securities, a very risky business worth hundreds of billions in the US, were turning bad.

The closing price of 2008 would be different.

The booming businesses across the world had a set of major setbacks.

The world, buoyed by vibrant stock markets, thriving economies and enormous consumer spending power, needed a factory that would produce for world consumption.

China, preparing for that role and jockeying for supremacy in that sphere for decades, ever since The Great Leap Forward, gladly grabbed the opportunity to be the factory of the world.

The mega brands of the West wanted cheap, timely and unhindered production, and China guaranteed that with their vast work force. Everyone was happy.

If China had become the factory—the producer—they had to have a customer service and back-office support nation. They needed them to efficiently handle the sales and services of the businesses and communicate to the world in fluent English. And that too, at a low price.

After the national shame of 1991, The Great Liberalization, envisioned, formulated and implemented by India's Finance Minister Dr Manmohan Singh, turned out to be for India what The Great Leap Forward was for China.

'No power on earth can stop an idea whose time has come,' said Dr Manmohan Singh, quoting Victor Hugo, while presenting the Union Budget on 24 July 1991.[7] These words signalled the start of the long and painful process of economic liberalization in India, which ended with great results.

---

7   ET Bureau, 'What Manmohan Singh Promised and What was Delivered', *The Economic Times*, 15 September 2011. Available at https://economictimes.indiatimes.com/news/politics-and-nation/budget-1991-what-manmohan-singh-promised-and-what-was-delivered/articleshow/9339032.cms.

The new policies integrated the nation into the global economy. They went against long-held convictions and discouraged public sector monopoly, encouraging competition in the market. This gave rise to a whole array of new companies that were able to showcase Indian entrepreneurship.

Foreign direct investment was flowing into India, and capital was no longer a restraining factor. This led to the burgeoning of homegrown private-sector companies that were professionally run—notably, the likes of Infosys and Wipro in the technology space and ICICI and HDFC in banking.

All this cumulatively unleashed a new energy into the entrepreneurial fervour of the Indian psyche.

The Y2K challenge was the litmus test of the Indian enterprise, which was just taking off.

India overcame the challenge successfully, with its software corporations providing the necessary call centre and back-office operations during that crisis. These were to be the customer service agents of the world.

If China was the factory, with a very savvy, English-educated, entrepreneurial workforce, India became the IT / Business Process Outsourcing/Call Centre of the world.

It created many opportunities, and Kerala, which had once missed the bus with its opposition to computerization, wisely stepped up and facilitated such businesses through clusters and infoparks.

In 2008, we established an IT arm and BPO in India, IPIX Tech Services, with partners Kavitha Gopan and Sreenath managing the business until Sreenath left and Kavitha took over.

As part of the promotions of that firm, we organized a mini-marathon in partnership with IIM-Kozhikode and the P.T. Usha

School of Athletics. Nearly 5,000 people and some celebrities attended the event.

While 2008 had opened with crude oil prices at a staggering US$99.67, outwardly displaying a vibrant financial ecosystem, there was massive trouble brewing in the US financial system. The first stirrings began in the summer of 2007, with the sub-prime loans and allied products. Although it was initially mostly confined to the US, as 2008 wore on, the gravity and scale of the losses were becoming obvious, and these would also have a sledgehammer effect on the global financial, economic and trade systems.

But the rise of the oil prices continued unhindered, touching an all-time high in June 2008 of US$148.93 per barrel.

While the oil prices were skyrocketing, there was another storm brewing beneath the surface. The scale of non-performing assets in the books of more and more banks worldwide were coming to the fore.

Major banks and financial institutions struggled to assess the value of the trillions of dollars' worth of now-toxic mortgage-backed securities that were sitting on their books.

By the summer of 2008, the scale of the carnage across the financial sector became apparent. Large banks were going down like ninepins.

IndyMac, a contraction of Independent National Mortgage Corporation, one of the largest savings and loan banks based in California, collapsed in 2008 and was seized by the United States Federal Deposit Insurance Corporation (FDIC). Two of the biggest US home lenders—Federal National Mortgage Association (FNMA), commonly known as Fannie Mae, and

Federal Home Loan Mortgage Corporation (FHLMC), popular as Freddie Mac—had been seized by the US government.

But the worst fears came true in September 2008 when the venerable Wall Street bank, Lehman Brothers, collapsed, marking the largest bankruptcy in the history of the US. Lehman Brothers became a symbol of the devastation caused by the global financial crisis.

The revered financial institution filed for Chapter 11 bankruptcy protection following the exodus of most of its clients, drastic losses in its stock and devaluation of assets by credit rating agencies, largely sparked by a loss of confidence, Lehman's involvement in the sub-prime mortgage crisis and its exposure to less liquid assets.

Lehman filing for bankruptcy is thought to have played a major role in the unfolding of the financial crisis of 2007–2008. With this crisis, sudden fear and uncertainty began to rule the markets and the mindset.

By the winter of 2008, the US economy was inextricably in the vicious grip of a full-blown recession. With a massive credit crunch, major financial institutions, predominantly in the US and Europe, were grappling with liquidity struggles, and stock markets around the world were in a free fall.

The bulls had retreated, far into the wilderness, beyond sight.

The bears were ruling the roost, strutting along on the street. The markets plunged even further after the 9/11 terrorist attacks.

The oil prices followed suit, invariably. From their stunning highs of US$148.93 in June, they nosedived to a nadir on 23 December 2008, scraping the bottom of the barrel at US$30.28.

It was a remarkable year of learning for me, too.

The year reaffirmed my belief in the need for diversification and the necessity to spread the hedges to mitigate concentration risk and hold a considerable reserve to stave off unexpected calamities like the one the world was witnessing.

These lessons and the mitigatory measures put in place across the Group would prove very helpful for the organization.

With very little exposure to the risky, toxic, distressed assets of the US banks, the Indian financial system was not directly impacted.

However, as the recession battered most major global economies, India also took a severe hit as investments and exports shrivelled.

According to World Bank data, India, which had been cruising at a 7.66 per cent growth in 2007, crashed to 3.08 per cent in 2008. The growth picked up again to 7.86 per cent in 2009 and then 8.49 per cent in 2010.

It was very obvious that owing to the very nature of its huge internal market and demand, India was a market and opportunity that should not be missed out on.

Like most countries in the world, the UAE was also adversely impacted by the global crisis initially.

But despite the global slowdown, the UAE swiftly adopted some economic, financial and monetary precautionary measures that cushioned the domestic economy and managed to contain the crisis without much knock-on effect.

By 2011, the nation had made rapid progress and businesses and investments were once again in the growth mode.

We also shifted gears into expansion mode.

In 2012, Morison Menon Hamriyah Free Zone came into being.

Not satisfied with sitting back and resting on laurels, ably supported by a collaborative team, we grew at a brisk pace, almost at the rate of a new branch every year since the new millennium.

With aviation, shipping and logistics being the key drivers of Dubai and the UAE economies, it was but natural that our next branch would be in the dynamic Dubai Airport Free Zone. The operations started in July 2013 with Biju Nair, who was promoted to Partner from Business Development Manager, at the helm.

CHAPTER THIRTY-ONE

Overcoming an Unprecedented Predicament

The EU Challenge

THE FOURTH OF DECEMBER 2011 started like just another busy day at the office. By mid-morning, all hell broke loose.

A client of our Sharjah office informed the Branch Partner Saju that Morison Menon had been included in an EU list of companies accused of being 'involved in the nuclear or ballistic missile programmes of the Islamic Republic of Iran'.[8]

I was aghast.

Upon obtaining more information regarding the matter, we learnt that the list had been issued by the EU on 2 December but,

---

8   *Official Journal of the European Union—regarding the sanctions against IRAN.* (EU) No 961/2010.

probably because of the UAE National Day weekend, we became aware of it only on 4 December.

Absolutely confident that the organization had done no wrong, the senior team and I, who had gotten together for a huddle, decided that it must have been an inadvertent mistake by some EU bureaucrats and that they would do the needful to correct it.

Our conviction was unshakeable. We were not going to be overly worried about the incident. The firm went about its regular work, the episode not impacting us in any way.

But then news about the episode began to appear all over the media, and I realized that even though we were innocent, being implicated in the matter would do serious damage to the firm's carefully and painstakingly built reputation and could also negatively impact the business.

We could not rest on optimism and complacency. We had to move fast to stem the damage.

Some of our bankers, not wishing to be seen having financial transactions with a firm on an EU sanctions' list, gave us a bit of breathing time, but after that froze our accounts.

Our operations were being hampered.

A few banks who knew us, our professionalism and adherence to the highest standards of ethics were prepared to support us further.

Things were getting serious. We could not take this lying down; we had to fight this injustice tooth and nail.

We convened an internal partners' meeting to analyse the issue in detail and created a core team of partners consisting of Khalid, Sudhir, Pushpan, Saju and myself to look into various ways to mitigate the damage and to design a strategy to clear our name as soon as possible.

The next logical step was to find the best available legal team and recourse in Dubai and then chart the way forward.

A meeting with a leading law firm in the UAE confirmed our worst fears. The matter was quite grave and could have serious business implications. As a first step, we immediately lodged a complaint with the EU. But that seemed to have fallen on deaf years; it produced no results.

With the matter sub-judice in the jurisdiction of the EU, they advised us to contact the reputed law firm Stibbe in Brussels, Belgium, which would proffer the best legal advice.

Stibbe, who operate through their main offices in Amsterdam, Brussels and Luxembourg together with branch offices in London and New York, are a full-service law firm with an internationally oriented commercial practice and a history going way back to 1911.

After initial discussions, we formally engaged Stibbe on 12 December 2011 to take up the case and represent Morison Menon Chartered Accountants before the General Secretariat of the Council of the European Union.

In parallel, we also put the excellent relationships that we maintain with the embassies and consulates of the EU countries in the UAE to good use.

Sudhir got in touch with the ambassadors and consulate generals of the UK, France, Germany and all the prominent countries in the EU.

We had several rounds of meetings with them to clarify our point. All of them were very supportive as they all understood our case well and quickly came to the conclusion that we were mistakenly implicated in the list.

Signing on Stibbe was a morale boosting move. We were absolutely confident that we had done no wrong and the Stibbe lawyers provided additional assurance and impetus.

Now we felt ready to take on the might of the EU.

Stibbe had handled many such cases successfully and their experience and bullish approach energized us, too.

So, from the initial state of shock and despair, with resilience and the force of conviction, we were now sure that victory would be ours in quick time.

Once again, our self-belief that we had done nothing unfair or unethical, that we had been wrongly implicated and that we would win the case was skyrocketing.

Before appealing the case, we wanted to know why we were falsely entangled in a case with such serious international ramifications.

By now, all the bad press about the affair had had its negative effect, too.

Although we did not lose many clients—they trusted our very high standards of professionalism and knew that we would never be involved with any illegal practice—we took minor hits, as was to be expected.

A few days had passed since the episode began.

We were very keen to know exactly what had happened. Slowly, the facts began to emerge.

The EU had launched sanctions against Iran over allegations that it was pursuing a state-backed nuclear weapons programme and they were monitoring companies that were trying to work around the embargo.

One such company under the radar was a shipping line and we were accused of being a front either owned or controlled by that state-backed organization.

We were obviously innocent and had nothing to do with being a front for anybody. It emerged that our actions had been misconstrued.

Morison Menon had assisted the shipping line to set up a company in JAFZ in our professional capacity and as part of our company setup services. This was much before the EU sanctions came into effect.

Even when we were in the midst of the issue, JAFZA did not consider the shipping line a violator of international laws and did not have any legal issues with them. The same shipping line facing issues with the EU was functioning normally in the free zone without any interruption.

It was a mistake by the EU. If they had shown due diligence or discussed the matter with us before imposing the restrictions, we could have explained the situation clearly and avoided the damaging incident.

Just because that organization was on the sanctions' list and because we had helped them to set up a company in the UAE in full compliance with the nation's rules and regulations, we were also included in the list of the EU, without any prior warning or notice.

In February, as recommended by Stibbe, we made our first move to appeal and applied to the Court of Justice of the European Communities to have our name removed from the Council of European Union list.

But our application was dismissed by the Luxembourg court.

As Plan B, preparing for the worst, we also floated a second company to ensure business continuity. It was set up in March.

Despite the setback, our lawyers were confident.

As advised by Stibbe, we appealed again to the higher courts.

By this time, our efforts through the embassies of Europe had paid off somewhat and the EU had realized that they had committed a mistake.

The sessions and hearings went on for two months and, following thorough investigations, the court, completely convinced of our innocence and non-complicity in the matter, officially removed Morison Menon from the EU's blacklist on 23 April 2012, declaring that there were no longer grounds for our inclusion in the list.

On 24 April 2012, the Official Journal of the European Union published the good news. We were thrilled. We had taken on a giant and cleared our name. It was time to take stock of the damage, regroup and focus again on growth.[9]

We had not lost many clients, other than a few in DIFC. Most of our clients were prepared to wait until we had cleared our name and emerged victorious.

However, had the case stretched on for another three to six months, we would have lost a majority of our clients and our reputation would have been irreparably damaged.

Initially, we wanted to file a case against the EU, seeking compensation for tarnishing our reputation and causing damages to our business.

---

9   COUNCIL IMPLEMENTING REGULATION (EU) No 350/2012 of 23 April 2012 implementing Regulation (EU) No 267/2012 concerning restrictive measures against Iran.

But after consultation with the lawyers we decided that Stibbe would take up the issue directly with the EU headquarters in Brussels.

In December 2012, we had decided to seek compensation and argued for the same from the EU. Citing precedence, they agreed to pay only about half of that amount.

To contest that we would again have to wage a legal battle with the mighty organization.

Therefore, after much deliberation, the senior management team unanimously agreed not to pursue the matter. We realized that the time and effort spent on legal challenges could be better utilized for more productive initiatives.

That difficult chapter was finally behind us.

CHAPTER THIRTY-TWO

Swanky New Head Office, New Brand Affiliation

THE EXPANSION DRIVES, INITIATED almost from the first day of the inception of Menon & Associates, continued non-stop over the next 15 years. They had brought us to a position where we were up to the brim of our capacity in our offices in Gulf Towers, our home for around 14 years.

Now there were only two options open: rent a bigger office space that could comfortably accommodate all existing personnel and also have enough buffer for future growth, or acquire our own.

Swanky new office towers were springing up all over Dubai.

Some of the best names in the world of architecture—individuals and firms—were blazing new trails in the fertile land of Dubai, breathing life into the immortal words of the great German poet Johann Wolfgang von Goethe, 'Music is liquid architecture; Architecture is frozen music',[10] or those of the great American architect and designer, Frank Lloyd Wright, 'Every great architect is—necessarily—a great poet. He must be a great original interpreter of his time, his day, his age'.[11]

In Dubai, as with almost everything, when it came to deciding on the new office, we were spoilt for choice. There was an array of stylish, posh buildings on offer. But we opted for an off-plan project available for purchase in Business Bay.

Today, when I look at our office on Level 15 of Lake Central, Marasi Drive, Business Bay, I know I made the right choice.

On one side we have the gleaming beacon of success and achievement, a modern-day commercial totem of what big thinking and big dreams can achieve, the shimmering tower of diamond, Burj Khalifa, always flashing a warning, reminding that there is much more to do and achieve.

And on the other, we have the Dubai Canal, a serene, sparkling body of water, at once soothing and seemingly still, yet gently traversing from the source to the destination, casting a shy glance at the suitors seeking her hand, beseeching her to stop, but non-committal as she continues, only for her destination to become the source in a continuum, from where the onward journey begins again.

I thought both views and landmarks defined me and my life, in a way. A sort of yin and yang.

---

10 Johann Wolfgang Von Goethe, Quotes, Quotable Quote, Goodreads. Available at https://www.goodreads.com/quotes/337462-music-is-liquid-architecture-architecture-is-frozen-music.

11 Frank Lloyd Wright Quotes, BrainyQuote. Available at https://www.brainyquote.com/quotes/frank_lloyd_wright_127723.

We love each and every nook and corner of the 12,300 square feet expanse.

The interior designers did a great job in creating an aesthetic, ergonomic office space, a comfortable workspace for our workforce.

The whole team moved in on 15 September 2014. Morison Menon, Level 15, Lake Central, Marasi Drive, Business Bay, Dubai would be the new address of the Group's Middle East HQ.

Every time we are in the office, we are swept off our feet by the airy, spacious new office, its positive energy, the natural light flowing in undeterred from all sides, the towering spire on the one side, the reflective lake on the other and the overall soothing colour schemes.

Once in a while, I stand by the window and stare homewards. I know it is a straight line back across the Arabian Sea to Edavilangu, where it all began. I never forget my roots. They further motivate me.

Motivated and in keeping with our rhythm of expansion and enhancement, in 2015, we moved the Abu Dhabi branch to a new state-of-the-art office in Abu Dhabi Plaza Tower on Najda Street.

The next year, we expanded further in Abu Dhabi, setting up a new branch in Khalifa Industrial Zone Abu Dhabi (KIZAD), the Emirate's first integrated trade, logistics, industrial and free zone which was announced in November 2010 by Abu Dhabi Ports and officially opened in September 2012.

In the same year, we also moved our JAFZA branch to a larger office on the 12th floor of JAFZA One—Tower A.

But the biggest transformation was to happen in January 2019.

After an 18-year-long, fruitful partnership with Morison KSi, a global association of professional service firms with over 150 member firms in more than 80 countries, we parted amicably, our intention being to enhance our level to a network membership.

With further growth ambitions envisioned, I was sure that the next stage would involve our transformation into being a network partner.

Prestigious clients such as large banks and multinational corporations would prefer to deal with networks and not associations, and that was becoming a stumbling block on our growth path.

Banks also play a huge role in determining who is empanelled for prestigious projects and clients, so it was becoming imperative to be enlisted in their priority category, and the upgradation to a network would help in that endeavour.

By becoming part of a network, there was also built into that relationship a stricter, assured quality control factor that was a big plus for the large clients.

Moreover, there would be considerable value creation and addition in upgrading to a network, and that would definitely bring along more business opportunities.

This decision, brainstormed by partners and agreed in consensus, was taken so as to move from an association to a network of firms that is a member of Forum of Firms, a partnership that would help the company gain access to the knowledge and resources of the new associates.

The next step was to evaluate the available network options and finalize the one that was most compatible.

We looked at several options. The challenge was to identify the right partner because most UAE firms already had associations and there were few options left.

Kreston International, the 13th largest accounting network with over 200 member firms employing over 23,000 professionals across 700 offices in 125 countries, was the obvious choice for various reasons.

One of the clinchers was that Liza Robbins, with whom I had had a great relationship when she was heading Morison KSi, was the new CEO of Kreston Global. That made integrating into the network even easier.

Moreover, with a large percentage of Kreston members (around 60–70 per cent) being big entities, we would have access to global knowledge and resources.

That was a significant advantage.

With the new affiliation, there were to be structural changes in the organization, with disassociation from the existing operations in Qatar and Oman.

However, there were to be no changes to the UAE management team.

Now, Kreston Global is ranked sixth in the UAE Networks Ranking of year 2020 by the International Accounting Bulletin.

In November 2018, our branding team was busy changing the website, name plates, letter heads and all the allied collateral. Our signage vendors fixed new signboards at our Business Bay office and all our nine offices across the UAE. It read: Kreston Menon.

The official launch event had 1,000 people in attendance, along with the heads of the UAE government, trade missions and other dignitaries.

CHAPTER THIRTY-THREE

When a Part of You Vanishes

ONE OF THE WORST nightmares for a person is the heart-wrenching news of the passing of a loved one. When you are least expecting it, it hits like a thousand sledgehammers.

It is especially so for the expatriate who is left to bereave thousands of miles away, with a million images of the dear departed passing through a numb mind, and searing pain tearing at each and every part of the body. You are consoled by friends and neighbours in a foreign land when your close ones are lamenting on their own, at home.

You want to be with them, but then there is a painful wait till the formalities of travel and its logistics are sorted out, and when you finally reach the doorsteps of your home, it is now missing one of its principal personae.

Each second and minute is a dagger painfully tearing out your innards.

These days, with the advent of social media and other technologies, communications with family and friends are almost an hourly occurrence.

Through chats and messaging on the various platforms, there is constant connection.

But back in the early 2000s, telephones were the medium of instant connection; Friday was the day most people devoted for staying in touch with family and friends, with the calls lasting for hours.

The day of 22 June 2001 was one such Friday. Aravind had turned four.

In our spacious Oud Metha Road apartment, we had organized a little party and invited some of our close friends over.

I had called home and spoken to Achan and Amma at length. Then Girija came on the line, also exchanging pleasantries and news about the latest mischiefs of Aravind and little Madhav, who was three months short of his first birthday.

Then Girija called her parents and spoke to them at length, most of it again devoted to news about the children.

Then her Amma mentioned that she and Geetha's son Sanjay would be travelling to Tirur on the Mangalore–Chennai Mail, popularly known as Madras Mail.

By late afternoon, the breaking news on Malayalam TV channels shattered our peace and sanity.

As more details trickled in, we were stunned.

We were praying fervently to all the Gods above, hoping against hope.

Then the painful specifics and more information began to emerge, further wrecking us.

The Kadalundi train disaster was one of the biggest accidents on the Indian railway network.

Around 5.15 pm in the evening, while the train, chugging towards Chennai, was crossing Bridge 924 over the Kadalundi river, connecting Malappuram and Kozhikode districts near Kozhikode, six carriages derailed and three plunged into the river. The bridge was situated near Kadalundi railway station.

The death toll rose steadily as bodies were retrieved from the wreckage over the course of a week. Fifty-nine people were eventually reported as killed or missing, including at least eight women and two children. Between 117 and 300 were injured and moved to nearby hospitals.

By dusk we learnt that Amma and Sanjay had met with a very tragic end.

I was shattered. Girija was inconsolable.

Soon, we flew home to join the rest of the family in one of the darkest moments of our lives.

Six years later, I was to undergo the same trauma that Girija went through. On 31 July 2007, my Achan moved on at the age of 77.

But for me the real devastation was on 7 April 2017 when my Amma left us. Amma had been my everything.

From very early on in life, my life was closely linked to that of Amma's. Whenever Amma moved to a new job, I would accompany her.

For me, she was a constant provider, guardian, guide, mentor and role model. In short, the personification of everything good, benign and kind.

I modelled myself after her.

So when Amma left us for good in 2017, aged 80, it was as if a part of me was lost forever.

I was in deep distress for weeks.

Gradually, time the healer worked its magic and calmed me down, at the same time further inspiring me to do even more to put into practice all the wisdom and lessons I had imbibed from her.

Our connection to that generation was finally severed when Girija's father breathed his last on 29 April 2019 at the age of 94.

Their memories and values will forever be part of our beings.

We also make it a point to recount to and reinforce in our three children and our nephews and nieces the invaluable, priceless examples they set by their lives.

Both Girija and I are thankful that we could surpass their expectations, give them the love and care they greatly deserved and make their wishes come true.

I cannot but relish the times we spent together, especially with the two of us and the kids in Dubai.

We cannot but thank them from the bottom of our hearts and remember them with gratitude.

CHAPTER THIRTY-FOUR

Obeisance to Society
Personal and Familial Social Responsibility

LONG BEFORE TERMS SUCH as philanthropy, altruism, charitable acts and Corporate Social Responsibility (CSR) came into vogue and I was even vaguely aware of them, I grew up observing them in action, learning how they were executed with empathy and respect, and admiring it.

There was only one guru, one exponent, one crusader I learnt from—Amma. Every day I witnessed an act of unconditional love, of limitless generosity, expecting nothing in return. So it was hardwired into my psyche, my nature and my very being.

I have seen tired, worn-out, worried faces break out into a warm, genuine smile when Amma's helping hand touched them. I have seen the gratitude in their eyes, and I hoped that one day I could spread the same goodness.

More importantly, I observed how a small act of kindness could be like a huge lottery for someone who is the beneficiary of such largesse.

Even during my early days, when I did not possess very much, I used to help as many people as I could, in any little way I could.

Therefore, when I was blessed with enough to contribute much more to the well-being of others, my first priority was to help those from my childhood—my relatives, friends, their families, neighbours—a lot of people who were part of my early life.

For I knew how one small act of kindness could be transformative for that person and the whole family.

So my earliest acts of CSR after I started earning were to create opportunities for people known to me, so that they could in turn ensure the well-being of their families.

That would be a force multiplier.

And from my early tough days, I knew many people who desperately needed help. A lot of my staff are from Cheekilode, Kodungallur and around Kozhikode.

Those who were qualified and educated were given appropriate positions in my company. I often gave them a slight edge in the recruitment process, knowing well that they might not be as adept or sharp or communicative as other aspirants from larger cities and towns but had the fire and qualities in them to do well and succeed.

If I knew people who were not academically oriented or qualified, I would appoint them as office boys or drivers, and if they showed the eagerness and aspiration for moving up in life, they would be given the required helping hand, especially in terms of training and mentoring.

Several of my accounting staff, all excellent performers, are people I have selected and brought in from the villages of my childhood.

Since there was a limit to how many I could directly employ within the Group, I also sought ways to find them jobs with companies that I helped start.

A lot of people from Cheekilode, Kodungallur, Kozhikode, its surroundings and other places that I have lived in during my early days have thus been employed in ventures we helped start, especially in free zones like JAFZA, which needed a lot of manpower.

Thus, I consider myself blessed and fortunate to have had a significant positive impact on the lives of individuals who have thereby been able to turn the fortunes of their families.

Amma has had her impact on me even in these acts of goodness.

When Amma knew that I would be coming home for a break, she would deliberately spread the news to those who needed help and had approached her earlier, so that they could time a visit to meet me directly and present their case in person; thus I was forced to listen to their pleas and do the needful.

I would help them as much as possible, wherever possible.

Amma had also pushed the cases of some people, after which I could not refuse them. There are about four to five people in my office, employed thus on Amma's recommendations.

I am also aware that there are a lot of unfortunate people who, due to reasons beyond their control, have been dealt a very unlucky hand. Some through terrible misfortunes badly need financial help.

I remember vividly the case of a close childhood friend. He was a well-built, tough guy, a very aggressive person right from our early days. After I left Cheekilode I had lost all touch with him and completely forgotten about him. Once, while on a brief visit from Dubai to our Cheekilode house where Unnikrishan Chettan was now staying, I went out on a walk, as was my usual practice.

Normally, I would walk out of the gate, turn left, do a brisk 30-minute walk and return.

On that particular day, as if by some strange instinct, I turned right instead and a couple of kilometres later, I had a feeling that I was on the path very close to my friend's house.

The whole neighbourhood had changed and hesitantly I went to what I thought was the house of one of my very close friends.

I called and my friend's mother responded, coming out to meet me.

She invited me inside and I was shocked and distraught to see my friend bed-ridden, weak and emaciated.

He told me how he had a stroke one day and had been confined to the bed for a long time after that.

Still, displaying a lot of brashness and arrogance that had been his hallmark in the younger, healthier days, he would approach the government to derive all the benefits that disabled people like him were eligible for and would acquire a three-wheeler, which helped with his mobility.

Despite all that, with him being the sole breadwinner, the family was in great financial distress.

What had happened to him was heartbreaking. I promised to help him.

Right away, I arranged to give him and his family a substantial sum to help tide over their immediate financial difficulties and assured him of our support towards the education of his children. I still continue to support him.

There are many more such people whom I have been supporting financially for nearly two decades.

I have entrusted a signed cheque book with my good friend Dileep Kumar, a CA who runs his own practice in Kozhikode. In consultation with me, he issues cheques as and when required to deserving people. Earlier, I used to issue advance cheques, but I came to know of people misusing them and therefore discontinued that practice.

Always grounded in reality, I am painfully aware that there are a lot of small institutions doing yeoman service taking care of the sick, disabled and elderly—those in dire need.

Probably because of Amma's influence and attitude, I can never say no to people who need help. Even if it is on an institutional level. When somebody approached me seeking help for such an institution, I just could not refuse them.

While on yet another holiday, Satheeshan, my friend from my B.Com days, who was handling the accounts for an old age home in Kozhikode, visited me at home and described the very tough situation the institution and its inmates faced. He invited me to visit them. I did. Again, it was heart-rending.

There were a lot of elderly people, around 50 men and women in total, in that retirement home. It was a ramshackle old building made of mud plaster—which is a mixture of heavy clay and water, containing chopped straw or manure to improve its mechanical strength when dry, and is used as a cheap material for construction when costlier alternatives are beyond reach—with a thatched roof.

Set in the midst of a beautiful compound with plenty of greenery, it seemed like a haven for the elderly people who did not have relatives or friends to take care of them.

The institution, through donations and help from well-wishers, was able to provide clean, nutritious food to the residents, but there were no facilities for some basic needs and entertainment and leisurely diversions.

Moved, I asked Satheeshan to provide me with a list of requirements and as needed immediately bought a few television sets and water beds, as many suffered from bed sores.

Once a month, a few leprosy patients would visit the old age home, and I also purchased a few essentials like blankets that they needed.

I also promised more financial help.

On my next visit—this was around 15 years back—I ventured into something bigger for the upkeep of the crumbling roof of the building. I hired an architect to inspect the building and find out what was necessary to repair the ceiling.

Termites, social insects, are a menace known for infesting and damaging home or property. And a swarm of termites, often called the 'silent destroyer' because they hide and thrive in homes or yards without any outward signs of damage, had eaten into the top structure of the old, mud-plastered building.

They thrive in the tropical weather of Kerala, which provides the right climate for them to flourish. The organic components of the plastering also provide the right matter.

There was only one way to save the building. We would have to completely reconstruct the entire roofing.

This was a very risky affair because the building was in a dilapidated state and there was a risk of it collapsing while the roof work was underway, and that was best avoided.

But the architect was confident that it was the only way the building could be saved. Therefore, we decided to go ahead with it.

He assiduously reconstructed the top of the building, putting in very strong wooden reinforcements—rafters, joists, struts and ceilings—wherever required and topped it with a new set of tiles.

The designer also added the necessary amenities, such as additional rooms and toilets, and by the end of the project, he had done a superb job of refurbishing a near-decrepit building into a new, strong modern structure.

Yet another occasion when I got the thumbs up and blessings from Amma was when I accomplished one of her long-cherished dreams.

With Achan and Amma being from Kodungallur, we have a large extended family there, all living around the ancestral family home. As part of the culture of having a family temple within the large compound around the house, we also had one, which was in a dilapidated state.

Knowing that Amma wanted to renovate it, I gave it a complete renovation and named it after Achan.

There was yet another temple that was very close to Amma's heart.

After I had built a house—I must in all modesty and humility admit that then it was quite palatial—in Kozhikode and Amma had moved there, it became a hive of activity.

Usually, people of lesser means are very hesitant to interact with the residents of opulent mansions as there is an inbuilt fear of rejection.

But Amma, being the simpleton, realist and skilled communicator that she was, knew that the trappings of riches and affluence mean little and that all human beings are equal and need to be treated with equal respect and dignity. She went out of her way to put people at ease.

So, far from being viewed in awe, people of the neighbourhood, rich and poor, would flock to our house and feel at home with Amma.

She also used to maintain excellent relationships with the authorities of the nearby Nellikavu temple.

After Amma left us in 2017, the whole neighbourhood was in shock and despair for a long time. They knew they had lost a genuine, caring, loving mother.

And when the temple officials approached me to redo the *aal thara* (several Kerala temples have a huge ancient banyan tree near them, around the base of which is a circular concrete seating arrangement, known as the *aal thara*, where people spend time socializing) of the temple, there was no need for second thought.

Knowing well about Amma's association with it, I was only eager to build the *aal thara* and it was named after Amma— Madhavathil Susheelamma.

I am very proud that it is not just me who tries to give back to the society. Girija also does considerable work in that area.

She is involved in a lot of initiatives, very quietly, without much publicity, mostly through her uncle who used to be a bank manager.

Always remembering her tough days, especially the financial difficulties when she was studying, she has made it a point to help people by financing their education and fulfilling the allied requirements. She also distributes lunch packets to destitute people on the roads in and around Kozhikode.

Before the pandemic, so as to reach the needy people sheltering in areas away from the glare of society, Girija's uncle would often visit these areas on a two-wheeler, since they are not reachable by car, and distribute food.

When Girija, caring and empathetic as she is, came to know about the phenomenal work being done by the Navajyothi Charitable Trust, Kozhikode, especially through Prasanthi Special School, she was immediately moved to contribute.

Initially, she provided financial aid and supported the dietary requirements by donating provisions and supplies.

When they requested help for constructing a classroom Girija, readily helped and named it after her mother.

Later, I also got involved with the Trust and sponsored the construction of the first floor of their new building.

Now we are very closely involved with their work and I have been made a Trustee. The Trust also runs the Prasanthi Rotary Centre for Slow Learners, Prasanthi Special Play School, Prasanthi Centre for Autism and Prasanthi Vocation Centre.

The Trust was started in 2000 by the Managing Trustee and Founder, Ramakrishnan Palat, upon finding that there were not many institutes for children with special needs in Kozhikode that were accessible to the financially backward sections. The Trust gives preference to such children at the time of admission and offers them 100 per cent free service.

To give more focus to our philanthropic efforts, Girija and I have started the CA Girija & CA Raju Menon Foundation, Kozhikode, Kerala.

We provide support for marriages, education and healthcare to individuals who approach us for help.

Women's empowerment is one of our areas of interest and we regularly conduct speaking/training courses for women aimed at enhancing their communication and public speaking skills.

We hope that, with the added confidence gained through such mentoring, they will come out and get more involved with civil society, increasing their level of participation and contribution.

Both of us wholeheartedly believe that all human beings are equal and equally capable of achieving and contributing to the community, society and humanity.

From a corporate point of view, I have made sure that as an organization we take Corporate Social Responsibility very seriously.

Kreston Menon conforms to the ISO 26000 Social Responsibility Standards, with Kreston Menon Chartered Accountants, Kreston ME Consulting and Kreston Menon Corporate Services implementing international social responsibility standards.

We conduct periodical evaluations through QS Zurich, the international certifying body, and they have certified that we comply with all ISO 26000 sustainability and social responsibility yardsticks.

We intend to carry on our personal and corporate initiatives with added zeal in the years ahead.

CHAPTER THIRTY-FIVE

Giving Back to Society
Corporate Social Responsibility (CSR)

KRESTON MENON PASSIONATELY BELIEVES in open-handedly giving back to the community in which it functions and thrives.

We are proud to be a corporate that started in the UAE and has emerged as a leading player in our extremely competitive field. Right from our beginning in 1994, we have contributed significantly to society through a multipronged strategy.

As a corporate that has thrived in this city and nation, we consider it a bounden duty to act as brand ambassadors for the nation at every opportunity that we get to facilitate foreign investments coming into the UAE and for UAE corporates and governments to function optimally in India.

As the UAE-based embassies, consulates, trade missions and international trade offices of countries and world bodies are the prime, productive conduits for the enhancement of business to and from the nation, Kreston Menon has proactively established close relationships with these key players and has initiated and maintained very active communications channels with them.

Internally, we have formed a pool of experts and advisors who will readily pass on their sound insight and awareness of business dynamics, requirements and opportunities to trade missions, as and when called upon.

Our broad range of experience and familiarity with the nitty-gritty in all matters related to setting up and efficiently running a company, gained over three decades, gives us a massive competitive edge over our rivals.

The embassies, consulates, trade missions and trade offices have, over the years, greatly appreciated our sincerity and commitment to the cause of furthering the UAE's business interests.

It is also significant that all this work is done pro bono, often with Kreston Menon spending significant amounts on producing and sponsoring the marketing collateral needed for such initiatives.

One such initiative that we are extremely proud of is partnering with the Expo 2020 team, as early as 2013, to support their bid to organize the world-renowned, unique and historic event in Dubai.

There was tough competition between Dubai and four other candidate cities bidding to host the Expo 2020—Ayutthaya (Thailand), Ekaterinburg (Russia), Izmir (Turkey) and Sao Paulo (Brazil).

As a proud Dubai and UAE company, we knew we had to lend our full support to the Expo 2020 bid and contributed by printing around 30,000 calendars for 2013 and distributing them widely across the governmental and semi-governmental organizations and corporates across the UAE as part of the publicity for the Expo.

When the winning city was announced in November 2013, after a vote by the 161 member nations of the Bureau International des Expositions—the international bureau responsible for overseeing the bidding, selection and organization of the World Expos—we were thrilled to have played our part in supporting Dubai's bid.

Our ties with these representative institutions and bodies are so valued that we are often requested to make presentations on doing business in the UAE to foreign delegations visiting the nation and to business councils operating here, which we do gratis.

With globalization and the ability to scale up globally being the key to growth and success in these times, like our in-country UAE expertise, we have also developed similar competence in the eminently complementary Indian market.

The highly efficacious and gainful UAE–India ties and trade relations go back a long way and are as vibrant as ever, so we partner with the UAE governmental arms and trade bodies to make inroads into the aggressive Indian market which boasts of a nominal gross domestic product (GDP) of US$2.87 trillion and purchasing power parity (PPP)-adjusted GDP of US$9.56 trillion.

Over the years we have been partnering with several governmental ministries, departments and bodies and have been present alongside them at premium international events like the World Free Zone Convention, UAE SME Awards Summit & Gala, UAE–UK Investment Summit in London, UAE–Asia

Investment Summit in Singapore and UAE–India Investment Summit in Mumbai.

As the free zones in the country champion investments and trade flow, and since we are closely involved with all such entities in the country, each of them, right from Abu Dhabi to Ras Al Khaimah, consider us as their active partners.

We consider it a privilege to have been present along with Abu Dhabi's prestigious Kizad Free Zone team at their first global launch in India and at a UAE–Korea Investment Summit in Seoul.

Similarly, Kreston Menon has partnered with the Dubai Airport Free Zone Authority, Ras Al Khaimah Investment Authority and Ras Al Khaimah Free Trade Zone at business meets with varied industry bodies in India.

We are active partners of the Vibrant Gujarat and Pravasi Bharatiya Divas, New Delhi.

As committed NRIs, we also associate very closely with the activities of the Indian Embassy in Abu Dhabi and the Indian Consulate in Dubai. To help the labourers move up in life, we have conducted training programmes in accounting.

We also used to do pro bono auditing for the Indian Community Welfare Committee for many years until they underwent restructuring.

It is our firm belief that the universities and colleges in the UAE are doing a phenomenal job in shaping the next generation of business and corporate leaders. As part of our initiatives to reach out to the students and university communities, our experts conduct guest lectures regularly at the Higher Colleges of Technology, including Dubai Women's Campus. We also invite them into our midst, giving them the opportunity to do internships and training with us.

Inextricably intertwined with the educational ecosystem of Dubai and the UAE, we had the honour and privilege to have a team from Dubai Women's College faculty spend six months with us to create two academic case studies. These case studies about Kreston Menon were then incorporated into give the business curriculum of the undergraduate International Marketing & Business course to provide a local perspective.

The first case study, titled 'The first Superbrand in the knowledge economy in the UAE: Kreston Menon in a mission of building better businesses globally', analyzes the company's unique journey to achieve 'Superbrand' recognition.

The second case study, 'The Superbrand Kreston Menon: Running economic and social engine together in the UAE', is an in-depth study of the company's initiatives towards a sustainable local CSR policy.

Contributing to the Emiratization drive of the government, we have a tie-up with the UAE National Students Training, through which we give the opportunity to interns from the Dubai Men's Campus and Dubai Women's Campus to work along with our staff, enabling them to gain invaluable insight into the actual workings of the auditing and consulting business and its associated verticals.

To cement our relationships with universities, partners at Kreston Menon act as complementary faculty at the Middlesex University Dubai Campus, S.P. Jain University and other such renowned educational institutions and have conducted guest lectures. We also host international executives who attend management courses at the University of Dubai while on exchange programmes.

Along similar lines, working with the Dubai Chamber of Commerce and Industry, we facilitate their country-to-country exchange programmes for international businesspersons.

In addition to the UAE universities and trade promotion bodies, due to the close ties we maintain with the embassies and consulates, several of them approach us to conduct training for students and executives who visit the UAE on familiarization trips.

When students of the University of St. Gallen were visiting the UAE, the Swiss Consulate reached out to us and our staff gave them a comprehensive presentation on 'Doing Business in the UAE & Dubai', outlining the key, relevant details.

Notable in this regard also is our partnership with Singapore Management University.

Realizing that internships and jobs are top priorities for students, we have forged a partnership with the Association of Chartered Certified Accountants (ACCA) to be on their list of approved employers. The ICAI has approved the partners of Kreston Menon for conducting articleship training and we are also an authorized training employer of the Institute of Chartered Accountants in England and Wales (ICAEW).

Yet another area of focus is our community partnership programmes.

Our involvement with the Al Jalila Foundation, Al Noor Training Centre for Persons with Disabilities, Rashid Paediatric Therapy Centre, Dubai Autism Center, Dubai Center for Special Needs, Dubai Foundation for Women and Children, Make a

Wish Foundation, Red Crescent UAE and Indian Community Welfare Committee go back many years.

We have contributed in several ways to these organizations that do exceptional acts of kindness. We have offered financial support and have provided visibility for their activities in our newsletters and publications and through volunteering.

We have forged an association with Dubai Cares, the philanthropic organization working to improve children's access to quality primary education in developing countries, and created public awareness about the initiatives of that UAE-based organization. We printed and distributed 45,000 copies of a co-branded calendar detailing the activities of Dubai Cares in various countries to all major business houses and government offices in the UAE.

As part of our CSR initiatives, we partnered with 'My Community ... A City for Everyone', an initiative launched by His Highness Sheikh Hamdan bin Mohammed bin Rashid Al Maktoum, Crown Prince of Dubai and Chairman of the Executive Council, to transform Dubai into a disability-friendly city by the year 2020.

Under this partnership, we distributed 50,000 copies of Kreston Menon's corporate calendar for 2017, a desktop calendar featuring the different activities under this noble initiative.

As part of our CSR initiatives in India, we support Alpha Palliative Care based in Thrissur, Kerala, one of the major providers of home-based alleviatory healthcare in the world, offering palliative services to over 8,500 patients on any given day. Specially qualified medical professionals including physicians, physiotherapists and nurses provide treatment. There has been a groundswell of support from the local populace and hundreds of community volunteers provide additional psycho-social support to the patients.

To further complement and support all our initiatives with the various segments, we also provide the optimal marketing and communications reinforcement to create the required awareness and recall in our target universe. The spearheads of that effort include the *Doing Business In Dubai, Doing Business In Abu Dhabi* and *Doing Business In Fujairah* publications, which highlight the essentials needed for any investor or entrepreneur wanting to learn the intricate details regarding the processes, benefits and possibilities. They have been very well received and are offered complimentary to government departments, senior bankers, diplomats, trade missions, lawyers, business councils, etc.

Developments at Kreston Menon and trends within the industry make up the contents of *Kreston Menon News*, a print/digital/mobile quarterly publication of 40,000 copies each in English and Arabic circulated among the UAE Government ministries/departments, bankers, lawyers, media and to all verticals of the economy.

Our excellent media relations ensure that we are frequently quoted on matters concerning our industry.

CHAPTER THIRTY-SIX

Kindred Spirits

WITHOUT A SHADOW OF a doubt, I can vouch for the fact that Girija's support has played a significant part in my success.

She has given me the utmost freedom to manage my affairs—personal, familial and corporate—without any interference, despite her own CA and CIA qualifications.

It is all about our mutual respect, trust and confidence in each other. Both of us know that whenever required, the other will be ready to lend a helping hand and act as a sounding board. Until then, we have our own private space to peacefully manage our affairs or create opportunities.

I greatly value the support and contribution Girija provides—both at work and at home—and the very valuable additions she makes through her empathetic approach, handling ups and downs with equal poise and grace.

This was tested when she first joined me in Dubai, in our shared apartment. We were all apprehensive about how she would adjust.

There were initial uncomfortable moments. But once my hilarious set of friends set the ball rolling with some banter, and thus broke the ice, Girija quickly became the anchor of the house.

Her ability to be accommodative has always stunned and impressed me.

If she can easily adjust to a new situation with ease, she also has the inherent quality of staying away from business that does not concern her.

In my life I have seen so many partners—husbands and wives—having a vicious tendency to control their spouses, always wanting to keep a tab on the other. They watch their every movement, keep tabs on their financial transactions, interfere in official decisions and constantly nag for attention.

I have been very lucky in that regard. Girija never interferes with the financial transactions, deals or arrangements the firm enters into. Neither is she keen to know about my personal investments, savings or to whom I give my money. She wholeheartedly believes that I have the right to control the wealth I have made.

I reciprocate. I do not ask about how she uses the fortunes she has made by dint of very hard work. I fully believe it is for her to enjoy the fruits of her labour. Over these years, I have come to recognize that deep within her is a sleeping giant, one that can be awoken at any required moment.

That is a great source of strength that I rely on, too.

I am extremely confident that she is a very capable leader who is exceptionally hardworking, extremely bold, immensely effective and eminently knowledgeable. She can easily step up and take my position any time as and when required, in case of any foreseen or unforeseen eventuality.

Very sound in her subjects and trades and well abreast of all the latest trends and developments, she is a natural paladin who, if and when called upon to lead, will take to the helm with ease, command respect and marshal the forces like a true champion.

I can envision that. I can see her move in deftly and quickly into the hot seat when required.

As a leader running a dynamic business that employs almost 500 people who are also breadwinners taking care of their families, that assurance of business continuity gives me a lot of peace of mind.

But right now, I am extremely confident that with me in charge she has no interest in the inner workings of the business or the strategic or tactical decisions and moves of the organization. I know well that all partners are extremely capable of managing their verticals and units and it is all working perfectly like a well-oiled machine.

Another trait that I admire in her is the quality to keep matters of home, family and work completely different silos—each has a separate space and they are never mixed.

Currently Girija works as Audit Partner at Kreston Menon, and she never discusses the work or the other partners, managers or senior staff with me.

That I think is an amazing quality, one that helps maintain very cordial familial and work atmospheres as there are no prejudices or preconceptions to judge any member of the team, and merit is the only yardstick of performance.

This is a rarity in private, family-run businesses and I think a lot of the credit for that goes to Girija, who maintains a very neutral, objective, meritocratic stance while in the office, which is very visible and palpable for all, and hence runs like a leitmotif throughout the organization.

Being a long-serving employee and senior partner, she either resolves all professional matters herself or, if and when required, collaboratively through discussion and deliberations with other concerned senior partners.

This deliberate separation of work and home also continues while we are at home. As its natural extension, never holding any office-related discussions at home has been a long-standing practice.

That is a great way to keep office matters in the office and never carry them home to vitiate the atmosphere there as it impacts quality family time and also unnecessarily causes tension and worry, which is detrimental to both health and sound decision-making.

The great upside is that we have peace of mind always.

This no-interference attitude of hers makes me feel responsible to take ideal, carefully thought out decisions, which turn out to be successful.

This is especially true of the new projects that I venture into.

She never asks me anything related to any new initiative I am working on. But if I do speak to her about such a plan, she will listen carefully, absorbing all the details in her sharp mind, probably even questioning some of the intricacies, but she will never give any comment that can hamper my idea of the venture.

In a way her attitude has contributed a lot to our organization, because she is also adept at ignoring immaterial comments and irrelevant non-issues raised by some members of the senior team, knowing well that they would not create any material dent to the organization.

It takes a person of extraordinary character and grace to maintain such a nonchalant approach.

I strongly believe that this unique disposition of Girija is one of the key factors that has helped me and the organization to bring together some of the best minds available to create an excellent senior team heading various verticals and to ensure that they stay with us for a considerable time.

Many of my senior team have been with us for 10–20 years and even more, a rare phenomenon, which is not very common in other similar organizations.

I have seen a lot of family businesses fragment in no time due to the unprofessional interferences, unnecessary interventions and messy meddling of family members.

I consider myself very lucky that I have been saved from such blushes.

All the partners are also well aware of Girija's inner strength and capabilities, and there is a very healthy mutual respect, which augurs well for the future of the organization.

But I am sure that a lot of clients and people who have interacted with her would mistake the calm, quiet and almost self-effacing behaviour as a sign of weakness or meekness, and as one who loves to be away from the limelight, I am sure she passionately treasures the inconspicuousness, too.

I smile to myself when I sometimes imagine the surprised faces of some such people upon seeing Girija as the leader they never knew existed.

Having lived together for nearly 30 years and faced so many thrilling ups and gut-wrenching downs, she fully trusts me in all decision-making—be it official, familial or personal. She is confident and knows well that I am very objective and dispassionate and value fairness and integrity above all else and that I would handle matters ensuring the benefit of all employees and family members.

Family is always her top priority.

At a time and age when a lot of qualified women are concentrating more on their work and career, often neglecting the very important, arduous and responsible task of nurturing children, Girija has always taken it upon herself to be a dedicated mother and homemaker.

The same is the case when she is at work, too. She gives her maximum possible dedication to the task at hand, working very late into the night, especially during audit season.

Her dedication to the profession and commitment to quality can be gauged from the fact that despite her CA qualification, she went on to do a Certified Internal Auditor certification from the Institute of Internal Auditors, USA, and qualified in 2001. CIA is the only globally accepted certification for internal auditors.

I remember the early days of Menon & Associates when she would be a completely dedicated auditor during the day and a tireless homemaker taking care of the infinite chores of the house in the evening.

When the babies came along, she considered her priority to be nurturing them, enveloping them in her love and continuous presence, often taking 6–12 months of leave, especially when each of them was in their early childhood.

Just as much as she loves them, Aravind, Madhav and Govind adore their mother.

Girija's constant presence and her love and attention have created a wonderful mother–children bond, and with me being away at work during most of their childhood, when business was at its booming best and needed my rapt attention, I felt like an outsider at times.

But boys being boys, with every passing year, they began to be increasingly drawn to me too, seeking my views and validation for their actions.

With the activities of the firm settling down into a business-as-usual mode, when they were into their teens, I had more time at hand to spend with them.

Our holidays, mostly to Kerala and other parts of India and sometimes to other destinations such as Europe or the US, would also prove to be occasions for great father–son bonding.

While I am grateful to Girija for her non-interference, I will also be eternally grateful to her— contrary to what I have been saying all along—for intervening and strongly urging me to adopt a course of action that may have been instrumental to the way things have panned out for us.

Just a couple of years into my career in Dubai, during my first job with Mak & Partners, I had a difference of opinion with the boss, Khalid Bhai.

Deeply disappointed with his attitude regarding a certain contentious issue, I got very upset and told him that I was quitting.

Our relationship being what it was, extremely warm and cordial, he would have immediately said no and asked me to reconsider the decision.

But someone in the organization had played politics and convinced him that I should not be pressed to stay and that if I wanted to leave, I should be allowed to go.

After that outburst about the acrimonious issue and the declaration of my intention to resign, when things had cooled down, I knew that it was a folly.

I had a good job and things were looking good. But there was nothing else that I had to fall back on. I had no savings. There were no alternate income streams. I was stuck.

In the evening when I got back home, I deliberated whether I should tell Girija about the incident. I decided to seek her counsel in the momentous decision.

After listening to the whole story, she told me her well-considered practical solution.

'Right now, without a Plan B, it would be foolish, almost suicidal, to put in your papers. I am not asking you to stay if you do not like the workplace anymore. There is no point in continuing in an organization if you cannot agree with your boss. You should leave,' Girija told me that tense night.

'But before you leave, we must have another alternative—another job or income stream that will help us survive. Otherwise it will be self-defeating and a mistake for which we will have to pay a big price. At this stage in our life, with so much dependent on your salary, we just cannot afford to give up in anger,' she added.

We deliberated for a bit longer that night.

Then she came up with this solution: 'Khalid Bhai has always been a loving father figure to you. So do not let your ego affect you. Go to him and say you are sorry, tell him that the outburst was a mistake and should not have happened and that you apologize and would like to continue. That is the best way to handle it.'

Then we switched off the lights and went to sleep over it.

Rested and at peace, when I woke up the next morning, I replayed in my mind the whole conversation of the previous night and concurred that her suggestion was the best way to handle the crisis.

As soon as office opened, I called Khalid Bhai and sought a meeting.

'I am busy, maybe we can meet in the evening,' came the reply.

I was getting tense now. Had he already made up his mind to let me go? Did he not want to meet me?

Putting those fears to rest, I got an appointment to see him, late in the evening.

So as advocated by Girija I climbed down quite a few notches from my aggressive stand the day before and apologized profusely for my anger, haste and resignation threat.

Khalid Bhai was a master at grandstanding too.

At once he transformed into generosity and magnanimity personified.

'No I never wanted you to leave. But when you said that you wanted to quit, I was very hurt and upset, and that is why I did not object to your insistence,' he confirmed.

With that one act of mine, things were back to the way they were between him and me.

I always wonder what would have happened had I not sought Girija's views and followed her wise advice.

Looking back, I hate to think what could have been our fate if indeed I had resigned.

She does not proffer advice often. But when she does, on a rare occasion, it is well worth a deep dive.

Seldom does she get involved with my decision-making process, and even more scarcely with financial matters.

But when she does make a judgement, I take her pointers very seriously. Especially regarding financial affairs.

She is extremely astute and observant and is capable of analysing matters very objectively and taking practical decisions.

On a couple of occasions, I have altered my stances after listening to her views, and the financial results have been beneficial. If I had not factored in her views, the outcome could have been a bit disastrous.

I am very lucky to have Girija.

As Amma would often say, she is also the best possible daughter-in-law for the family. For me, she is a true kindred spirit.

CHAPTER THIRTY-SEVEN

Yokoso to Japan

Three Musketeers, You Have Arrived

UNDER A SIGN READING 'Yokoso Japan—Welcome To Japan', at Narita Airport in Tokyo, stood the three musketeers of the family—Aravind, Madhav and Govind—beaming. Another sign near a flight information display systems board showed the time they had arrived and yet another at the baggage carousel indicated 'Arrived'.

Over the nearly three months that I took to compile all these thoughts and memories and put them down on paper, I scanned through a lot of pictures. Despite the pandemic, I also flew down to Kerala once after having taken the vaccine jabs. There I flicked through many photo albums, trying to remind myself of some of the scenes, images and events of my life vividly captured in film and stored for the future on photo paper.

There were many photos of the kids too, in different locales and all sorts of costumes—from Dubai, Kerala, India and other foreign tourist destinations.

But the pictures of the three from Japan were striking. They reminded me that, in a way, they had arrived. They were not the kids we always consider them to be, nor the way we parents want them to remain—kids. In seeking to travel alone, the three were breaking free from that eternal umbilical cord of loving control with which we parents always try to hold on to them.

The pandemic, which has decimated lives and livelihoods the world over, has also made us think deeply about how blessed and fortunate we have been to live in a safe and secure environment like we have in Dubai and the UAE. It has also given us a lot of surprise very-welcome family time together.

Aravind, 25, completed his Bachelor of Business Administration (BBA) degree from Amity University, Dubai, then did his articleship at Kreston Menon to acquire an Association of Chartered Certified Accountants (ACCA) qualification. He has completed all the requirements and is now a member of the reputed body. He is normally a busybody who hardly gets to spend much time with us. He is also training to qualify as an ICAEW Chartered Accountant (Institute of Chartered Accountants in England and Wales) and is now pursuing a Master's in Business Analytics at Exeter University, UK. COVID restrictions have forced him to spend more time with the family.

Madhav, a true millennium kid, was born in September 2000. He started his four-year BA in Accounting Studies at the American University in Sharjah, in 2018. He is scheduled to graduate in 2022 and plans to do his further studies abroad.

Meanwhile he is also undergoing a training programme at the PricewaterhouseCoopers' Academy to get his ACCA.

Govind, now 20, is doing the second year of the four-year Bachelor of Arts course in Accounting and Finance at Durham University, UK. He is also pursuing his ICAEW.

When spending time with them in the evenings and during weekends, I remember how when they were tiny tots in the early days and growing up with the inevitable cycle of life, I was spending considerable time at work growing and managing a business that was trying to maximize its potential. Once again, Girija, the very loving, caring, supportive and empathetic wife and mother, would spare no effort to make sure that the kids were nurtured in every possible way to shape them into physically, mentally, spiritually and academically adept children.

We made sure to give them every opportunity to learn about and value their roots, develop a close association with their uncles, aunts and cousins, be fluent in their mother tongue and proficient in all forms of its usage and relish the various rich cultures they were lucky to be part of, both Keralite and Indian.

Thursday nights in Dubai, when the weekend starts, were then and are even now reserved as family movie time, when all of us sit together to enjoy a Malayalam, Hindi or Tamil movie. They are a great way to expose children to the various diverse cultures and practices that abound in Kerala and India. Now that Aravind is a working man, he has moved out of our home film society, even though the remaining four members are as active as ever.

Taking a leaf out of her father's book, Girija abhors wasting time and has consistently made efforts to pass this trait down to the boys. From a very early age they were trained to do their laundry, help with chores at home and even help with cooking. While they are well-versed in handling all household chores, the one they have taken a great liking to is the art of gastronomy. All of us are gourmands—absolute, unabashed foodies. Girija and I are conservative in our tastes, mostly preferring Malayali and Indian food. The kids are as cosmopolitan as their friends in school and college.

Recognized globally as a very tolerant city and nation, Dubai and the UAE are home to people from around 200 nationalities who do business here or live here, or come to study or visit the UAE.

To cater to the diverse culinary demands of this vast and variegated national and expatriate population, the dynamic city and nation have restaurants offering a complete smorgasbord of cuisines. According to government statistics, there are around 12,000 restaurants and cafes in Dubai alone. So it is not surprising that the kids became foodies and also experimental chefs trying out their own cooking, especially on weekends. A training stint from childhood has ended up becoming a passion now.

In the summer months, the punishing sun beats mercilessly down on the sands of the Arabian desertscape, roasting the barren wilderness and imparting enough energy for its fine grains and particles to be kicked up. The vicious simooms then carry these particles into the towns and cities, worsening the situation already made intolerable by the grilling received during the long days and short nights.

Historically, to give the kids a break from their hectic studies and the punishing heat, schools have a summer break of over two months, usually around July and August. Classes resume only around late August or early September. During these two months

Girija would compulsorily take off from work and accompany children for their two-month kinship with the larger family. Extremely busy with work, I would try to grab a two–three-week holiday with them, usually spent in travelling to interesting places in Kerala, India or other popular global destinations.

While in Kerala, Girija would give them classes in instrumental and vocal music, training them on various instruments such as the tabla, *chenda* and keyboard. A lot of time would be spent with grandparents, uncles, aunts and cousins on both sides of the family, and the kids would also be introduced to the larger family—the great uncles and aunts and the second and third cousins.

From their childhood, our language of communication at home was always Malayalam, but since their lingua franca of life in school and college is mostly English, visits to Kerala would also help improve their Malayalam skills.

During these annual summer visits to Kerala, a superb time for kids as they get to enjoy 'God's Own Country', as the state is branded, with the natural splendour at its glorious best, the monsoon arriving in all its magnificent beauty. The brooks, streams, rivers and lakes would be full to the brim and often spilling over the banks, and all the shrubs, plants and trees would wear a garb of lush green.

But Girija would also expose them to the harsh realities of life.

She would make it a point to take the kids to homes for the unfortunate and the destitute and schools for the differently abled, which were harbours for people of determination.

The kids have become much wiser and more compassionate because of these visits with their Amma and are better able to understand the extremely fortunate circumstances they were born into. We hope they will continue the big-hearted traditions of their grandmother which we have strived to continue and take it upon themselves, when it is their time, to give back to society.

Girija and I have also taken pains to ensure that their physical capabilities are equally developed and toughened along with their mental and emotional strengths. At a very early age, they were literally thrown into the deep end of a pool to toughen their brains and brawn. Girija was dead set on teaching our boys swimming and also making sure they were physically very fit. Very early on, all three kids would take an early bus to their school to join the swimming classes.

All three turned out to be good at swimming, but Madhav and Govind were naturals and took to the pool like fish. They were so good that they represented the school many times at the swimming competitions in the Central Board of Secondary Education (CBSE) championships for national and international CBSE-affiliated schools in India. The CBSE is a national level board of education in India for public and private schools, controlled and managed by the Union Government of India.

Underscoring the importance of a well-rounded education, Govind often says that his swimming coach not only helped him swim but was also instrumental in him faring well as an all-rounder. Aravind and Madhav concur too.

The eldest, the undisputed leader of the team, always recounts how his teacher helped him fight fears and eventually turn out to be a voracious reader and an excellent communicator well versed with events in the world. I am often surprised at his awareness of the latest happenings, his strong, well-formed convictions, his sense of right and wrong and analysis of business trends. We often discuss matters of the day, and if I happen to talk about Bill Gates and what he does for philanthropy or Elon Musk and how his business decisions sometimes seem like that of a maverick, Aravind has such a ready, convincing response with enough of data to back it that I have to take a back seat. I am sure his natural head start in education and work have given him an edge over the others, but Madhav and Govind, keen learners and observers that they are, soak up a lot of tips from their leader. As they complete their education and begin their lives in the competitive world of work and business, they will also evolve as mature and astute professionals.

Girija and I have given them the freedom to bloom into confident, independent young men and are very proud that they have evolved so. We never forced them into any particular stream of study. But from very early on, they have been seeing and hearing of business terminology and news about developments, mostly related to auditing, accounting, finance and consulting, so it is only natural that they all took up the same line of study, which will help them pursue the same kind of careers of their parents. I am sure all the business talk at home helped form their choices.

In the early days, feeling guilty that I was not spending enough time with children because of work commitments, I decided to drive them to school. So they were asked to discontinue travelling by school bus, which they loved because they would have a lot of fun with their friends. They missed it a lot in the beginning. Maybe I was a little selfish, but I loved the prospect of spending more time with them.

So I became their chauffeur and the drives to school became a father–sons bonding time. Usually this was spent discussing matters of the world, business trends and strategies.

One of the things which I used to reinforce in the kids was that we parents would never force them to do anything, but to be successful it was a good idea to have a professional degree, like in engineering or in chartered accountancy. I always told them: once you have earned that degree and are still convinced that you want to pursue some other interest, rest assured that we will never force you into something that you do not like and will always support you.

I think the kids have got the message loud and clear. Those bonding drives have been an invaluable experience. They have helped us in such a way that I have become more of a friend than a father passing down orders to them. That open communication and affability have meant that if they have an issue, they feel free to discuss it with me as they would with a friend.

While in childhood they were clearly more attached to their mother, I guess the kids thought that they could identify more with and sought to fashion themselves along the lines of their father when they emerged from the safe cocoon of home and school into the real world. Their father's tougher experiences, fun and frolic in school and college and more manly pursuits such as his propensity for cars appealed to them. Most importantly, they dream of becoming successful entrepreneurs one day.

Girija says jokingly that the kids come to me for advice because they know that my ways are more lax, friendlier and flexible than hers, which they wrongly judge to be strict and rigid. But that is not to say that my views are considered sacrosanct.

They sometimes viciously tear down my arguments, treating me unkindly and labelling my ideas as stubborn, impractical and irrational. They blame me for a host of decisions, which in their opinion went wrong, again labelling them in unsympathetic terms. And if I counter, they will come back with plenty of data, examples and episodes such that I have to find an excuse and slip away.

No, just kidding, but we do very often have friendly, argumentative evenings at home.

One thing that Girija and the boys agree unanimously about is that I am mostly a cool, calm and collected person. No matter how serious or pressing the matters that bother me, I have over the years developed a mechanism to let go of it quickly. Even if it is a very grave office issue, I leave it back at the office and wipe it clean off my mind when I step out of the building. If it is a family-related anxiety, I immediately work on it, not allowing it to bother me. Come what may, when it is time to go to bed, I am at peace and hence always get a good night's sleep.

The children and I agree that Girija is the exact opposite, especially if the issue involves the kids and the family. She is nervous all day till a solution that meets her exacting standards is found, and if not, it stretches into the night and next day or until the desired end result is obtained. She tosses and turns and can't sleep a wink on such nights.

From my life experiences I know that we are all influenced by our role models. Directly and indirectly. Amma was the paragon of virtues for me, and I imbibed her kindness, empathy, caring and communication skills. Girija's idol was Achan and his hard work, discipline, strict routines and habit of never wasting even one nanosecond, which were the qualities imprinted on her mind.

While I am extremely happy about my professional and entrepreneurial advancements, what I am most proud of and infinitely grateful for is my family. I sincerely hope that going forward, the brothers emulate the best from our parents and us, and better it and do more. Most importantly, they should support each other and those who need it with a helping hand.

I hope Girija and I have motivated them enough to do this.

PART II
CODA

CHAPTER THIRTY-EIGHT

The View from My Perch

I AM ATOP YET ANOTHER perch as I write this.

The view from this perch of mine is as commanding as humanly possible, high up on one of the most magnificent, towering testaments of the possibilities of the human race and also reflecting the inordinate potential of Dubai.

Without any qualms, I will vouch that it is the amalgamation of both these dynamics that have helped me obtain this pied-à-terre on the Burj Khalifa, gloriously reflecting light on a sunny day and shining like a fiery torch of hope at night, its individual components cumulatively emanating radiance.

The boy whose life began in a tiny thatched hut in distant Kerala is grateful and feels privileged to own a piece of history, one inextricably intertwined with the Dubai mojo.

From here I have an unobstructed 360-degree view. I see the past, the present and the future clearly, unobstructed, and envisage that what lies ahead is also shaped here.

On a brilliant day, I can see across the seas and vicariously travel to my home village in Kerala, the villages, towns and cities that I have traversed, scan the educational and professional institutions that chiselled me into what I am, remind myself of the people who inspired me and the ambitions that drove me.

If I go to the floor-to-ceiling windows and look at the city, I can map the growth that this city facilitated for me in a glance— the small apartments in and around Deira, the bigger apartment buildings we moved into, the excitement of the kids as we moved into our first villa in Jafliya and then the many others we shifted to in the same area.

If I glance down in a southerly direction, I can see our house in Sobha Hartland.

When my gaze hovers over the city, the distant view helps me retrace my career here—the early offices in Hor Al Anz, Deira, Beniyas Square, the shift across the Dubai Creek to Oud Metha, and the long stay there.

In a south-westerly direction, Lake Central Tower, Business Bay, stands tall with Kreston Menon ensconced in it.

The past and present have been extremely kind and generous to me. Now it is the future that I look forward to. This time I am very keen to contribute, eager to spread goodness, prosperity, respect, care and dignity. I foresee several more years in the same mode, driving the business at the helm of Kreston Menon along with my colleagues and engaging in philanthropic initiatives— personal, familial and corporate.

Fortuitously, the children show a keen interest in the business and one is already initiated into it. I hope they will be able to adapt to the rapidly evolving business fluxes and stay ahead of the curve to ensure that Kreston Menon maintains its pole position.

It is my fervent wish that my boys, should they wish to continue with the firm, have the sagacity to learn from the senior partners and work harmoniously with their peers, at every moment safeguarding that objectivity, equity and fairness which are the keywords within corporate culture—one that I strived to enshrine as part of the ethos of the company.

Even if they are keen on furtherance, I will still be associated in a mentoring role.

Ideally, I would like to share my time between my existing ventures in Kerala and new initiatives in business and philanthropy that I plan to be involved with there and start-up projects in Dubai. I have the courage and confidence to do that 50–50 arrangement, shuttling between Kerala and Dubai, because Girija is keen to continue in Dubai, taking care of the children now as they find their way, providing all the warmth and shelter they need. I am sure she is also eagerly looking forward to them settling down with their own families, though there are still quite a few years for that.

I am passionate about developing a venture that combines a sustainable, not-for-profit business and a philanthropic initiative—a chain of pharmacies that will provide medicines for free or at low cost to the needy and deserving. Plans are underway to test it in Kozhikode city and then scale up as feasible across the district and then across the state. A word of caution: these are all still in the nascent stages—just a few sketches and lines on the drawing board.

Along the same lines and at a similar stage of development is the ambitious plan to provide basic yet tasty and nutritious meals to those in dire need through a chain of brick-and-mortar and mobile units.

On the for-profit side, tourism is an area that excites me. I see a huge potential for growth in Kerala, India and Dubai. And I can foresee a few profitable possibilities for connecting the dots on that triangle. I have a few outlines in my mind, and I am sure in the next few years I will breathe life into them.

As for the firm, we have learnt a few invaluable lessons from the pandemic. We can no longer afford to be comfortable with long-term planning and vision. Even if we have a directional roadmap looking far ahead, we have to be nimble and swift-footed to dodge the curveballs thrown at us and at the same time readily create new options and opportunities and agilely step up. This is necessary because scientists, thinkers, visionaries and futurologists warn us that the frequency of occurrence of cataclysms and pandemics could be hastened by climate change and the wanton destruction of nature and natural habitats. Equipping the firm for the short and medium terms, making sure that the systems and processes are robust, resilient, responsive and ready for unforeseen challenges and looking for ways to enhance our revenue streams and profitability consumes my mind now.

Eternally optimistic, I am confident of humanity's inherent goodness and ability to overcome setbacks and emerge triumphant. There is no doubt in my mind that the Gods above, who have been extremely generous to me and my family, will bestow even more of their boons upon us so that, in turn, these blessings can be used wisely to generate more wealth, multiplying it manifold so that it is invested for developing the business and altruistic initiatives further.

Good begets more good, as Amma has shown and my life experiences have proved beyond doubt. That is when life becomes even more beautiful, as many have shown through their illustrious lives, through the many tomes that have been written, the myriad songs that have been sung, and as the lyrics of that legendary song by the iconic singer say.

I put down my pen and look out from my writing desk. What a wonderful world.

That is the view from my perch.

Glossary

1. Corporate

Kreston Menon:

The group had a humble beginning in 1996 as the Certain Audit Bureau in Dubai, UAE, and have rebranded many times since. In 1999, they became Menon & Associates and in 2000 partnered with Morison International to become Morison Menon. After a long partnership with that global association of professional services firms, the group upgraded to a network status by forging an alliance with Kreston Global in November 2018 and changed its name to Kreston Menon.

2. Apparel

Mundu:

A garment worn around the waist in the South Indian states of Kerala, Tamil Nadu, Karnataka and Andhra Pradesh. It is normally made of cotton and is white or cream in colour. While men use this commonly, women wear it for festive occasions.

A similar apparel called the lungi, which is a colourful version of the mundu, is much more popular and is worn in varying styles across many Indian states and in the subcontinent.

Mundum Neriyathum:

Traditional clothing of the women of Kerala. The most basic traditional piece is the mundu, the lower garment, which is the ancient form of the sari. The neriyathu forms the upper garment for the mundu.

The mundum neriyathum consists of two pieces of cloth and can be worn in either the traditional style with the neriyathu tucked inside the blouse or in the modern style with the neriyathu worn over the left shoulder.

3. Cultural

Aal thara:

A platform built around a banyan tree, a common feature in many Hindu temples in Kerala.

Achan:

Father in Malayalam, a language spoken mostly by the people of Kerala and also south-western India, from Mangalore to Kanyakumari.

Amma:

Mother in Malayalam.

Ammumma:

Grandmother in Malayalam.

Chechi:

Elder sister in Malayalam.

Chettan:

Elder brother in Malayalam.

Kainottam:

Palmistry or palm reading in Malayalam.

Palmistry is also known as palm reading, chiromancy or chirology. It is the practice of fortune telling through the study of the palm and is prevalent all over the world, with numerous cultural variations.

Kakkathi:

In Malayalam, a female palm reader, one who belongs to a nomadic tribe of fortune tellers who practice palmistry.

Lakshman Rekha:

In India, this has religious references. Lakshman Rekha finds a mention in some later versions of the Ramayana, which is one of the two major Sanskrit epics of ancient India and an important text in Hinduism, the other being the Mahabharata. This is considered to be a red line of sorts, one which is not to be crossed come what may. It implies that one must abide by strict professional codes and not indulge in unethical practices. It is a strict convention or a rule, never to be broken. It is similar to the bright-line rule of the US constitutional law but has no legal locus standi.

Mana:

Mana in Malayalam refers to the house of the Namboodiris (the Brahmins of Kerala). Namboodiri homes have various names such as Illam, Mana or Madhom, with the distinction between them being unclear.

Onam:

Onam is an annual harvest festival celebrated by the people of Kerala. The date of the festival is determined using the Panchangam, the Hindu calendar and almanac, which follows traditional units of Hindu timekeeping and presents important dates and their calculations in a tabulated form.

Onam falls on the 22nd Nakshatra Thiruvonam in the month Chingam, which in the Gregorian calendar overlaps with August–September. It is celebrated to honour the mythical ruler, King Mahabali, who is believed to be much loved by Keralites for his kind heart and just rule. He is believed to visit Kerala on Onam.

Tharavad:

Malayalam word for ancestral home, usually used as the common house for the joint family system practised in Kerala.

Thiruvonam:

The most important day of the four-day Onam festivities is Thiru Onam or Thiruvonam, meaning 'Sacred Onam Day'. It is celebrated on the second day.

The First Onam, Uthradom, is regarded as Onam Eve. King Mahabali is believed to arrive in Kerala on this day. It is believed that the king spends the next four days in his erstwhile kingdom. It is a jubilant occasion when people rush to complete their Onam shopping—this last-minute dash for shopping is called Uthradappachil—and the cleaning of their homes. It is also an auspicious day for buying fresh fruit, vegetables and other provisions.

The Second Onam, Thiruvonam or the main Onam, is when King Mahabali is said to visit people's homes. Homes are spic and span, elaborate pookalams (an intricate and colourful arrangement of flowers on the floor) are laid, new clothes are worn and families gather to enjoy an elaborate vegetarian feast known as the Onam Sadya or Onasadya.

The Third Onam, Avittam, marks the preparations for King Mahabali's return to the heavens. The main ritual of the day is taking the Onathappan statue, which was placed in the middle of every pookalam during the past 10 days, and immersing it in nearby rivers or the sea. The pookalam is cleaned and removed after this ritual.

The Fourth Onam, Chathayam, marks the continuation of the post-Onam celebrations for the next couple of days with snake boat races, pulikkali (literally means 'the play of the tigers'; it is a colourful and entertaining folk art with men in tiger makeup and costumes) and related festivities across the state.

4. Culinary

Puttu:

A breakfast dish eaten in the South Indian states of Kerala, Tamil Nadu and parts of Karnataka, as well as in Sri Lanka. It is made of steamed cylinders of ground rice layered with coconut shavings.

Lentils:

Lentils (Lens culinaris or Lens esculenta) are edible legumes. It is an annual food crop. The majority of the world's production comes from Canada and India.

In cuisines of the Indian subcontinent, where lentils are a staple, split lentils are often cooked into a thick curry/gravy that is usually eaten with rice, rotis or other rice-based dishes.

Idli:

A type of savoury rice cake, originating from the Indian subcontinent, popular as a breakfast dish in South India and Sri Lanka.

Idli has several variations, including rava idli, which is made from semolina. There are many regional variants including sanna of the Konkan region of Karnataka.

Dosa:

A thin pancake or crepe, originating from South India, made from fermented batter predominantly consisting of lentils and rice.

Dosas are a common dish in South Indian cuisine. They are served hot along with chutney or sambar. Other accompaniments include chutney powder (a fine groundnut and lentil powder).

Vada:

Vada is a category of savoury fried snacks from India. Different types of vadas are fritters, cutlets, doughnuts or dumplings.

Popular in Mumbai.

Chaat:

A savoury snack from India, it is typically served as an hors d'oeuvre at roadside stalls or food carts across the Indian subcontinent, including India, Pakistan, Nepal and Bangladesh.

All chaat items are made from fried dough, with various other ingredients added to every item. The original chaat is a mixture of boiled potato, crisp-fried bread, gram or chickpeas and tangy-salty spices, with sour Indian chili and dried ginger and tamarind sauce, fresh green coriander leaves and yogurt for garnish.

Vada pav:

A vegetarian fast-food dish native to the state of Maharashtra. The dish consists of a deep-fried potato dumpling placed inside a bread bun (pav) sliced almost in half through the middle. Usually accompanied with one or more chutneys and a green chili pepper.

Panipuri:

Panipuri, also known as gol gappe, fuchka, gupchup, golgappa or pani ke patake, is a type of snack that originated in the Indian subcontinent and is one of the most common street foods in India, Pakistan, Nepal and Bangladesh.

Bhelpuri:

A savoury snack from India, it is also a type of chaat. It is made of puffed rice, vegetables and a tangy tamarind sauce and has a crunchy texture.

Sevpuri:

Sevpuri is an Indian snack and a type of chaat.

Dahipuri:

The dish is a form of chaat and originates from the city of Mumbai. It is served with mini puri shells (gol gappa), which are more popularly recognized from the dish panipuri.

Ragda-pattice:

A dish of mashed potato patties and gravy, it is part of the street food culture in the Indian states of Maharashtra and Gujarat. It is similar to chhole tikki, which is more popular in North India.

Pav bhaji:

A fast-food dish from Maharashtra consisting of a thick vegetable curry (bhaji) served with a soft bread roll (pav).

5. Geography

Villages, towns and cities from Raju's early life, mostly spent in northern Kerala.

- Aricode
- Balusserry
- Cheekilode
- Chelannur
- Edavilangu
- Kadungalloor
- Kizhissery
- Kodungallur
- Kolathur
- Koyilandy
- Kozhakkottoor
- Kozhikode

- Kunnamangalam
- Kuzhimanna
- Madappally
- Malappuram
- Payyoli
- Thamarassery
- Thrissur
- Vadakara
- Valavannoor

6. Historical

Bartolomeu Dias:

A Portuguese mariner and explorer who lived between c. 1450 and 1500, he was the first European navigator to go around the southern tip of Africa in 1488 and demonstrate that the most effective southward course lay in the open ocean to the west of the African coast. His discoveries effectively established the sea route between Europe and Asia.

Cape Verde:

Cape Verde, the westernmost point of Africa, is an archipelago and island country in the central Atlantic Ocean, consisting of ten volcanic islands. The Portuguese explorer Dias chose the name Cape Verde—Green Cape—because he saw that the islands had tall trees and lush green vegetation as he sailed past it.

Gandhiji:

Mohandas Karamchand Gandhi (2 October 1869–30 January 1948) is revered as the Father of The Nation in India. He was an

Indian lawyer who used peaceful, non-violent methods to lead India's struggle for independence from British rule.

Kappad:

Kappad, also known locally as Kappakadavu, is a beach near Koyilandy in Kozhikode district, Kerala, India.

Historically a very important place, it is where Portuguese explorer Vasco da Gama, the first European to reach India by sea, landed. The Government of Kerala has installed a stone monument to commemorate the landing, with the inscription: 'Vasco da Gama landed here, Kappakadavu, in the year 1498'.

Kappakadavu:

Another name for Kappad; see above.

Mahé:

Also known as Mayyazhi in Malayalam.

Mayyazhi:

Mayyazhi is a small town in the Mahé district of the Union Territory of Puducherry, also known popularly as Pondicherry. It is situated at the mouth of the Mayyazhi River, also known as Mahé River, and is surrounded by the state of Kerala with Kannur district surrounding it on three sides and Kozhikode district forming the other border.

Muziris:

With its exact location still not determined, Muziris was an ancient harbour and urban centre on the Malabar Coast, in the modern-day Indian state of Kerala, dating back to at least the first century BC. Though historians and archaeologists have not been able to pinpoint its location with any degree of accuracy, it is widely thought to be situated around present-day Kodungallur near Thrissur in Kerala.

Renowned as a key sailing hub, Muziris was instrumental in the trade between South India and Persia, the Middle East, North Africa and the (Greek and Roman) Mediterranean region.

Nehru:

Jawaharlal Nehru (14 November 1889–27 May 1964) was an Indian Independence activist and, subsequently, the first prime minister of India, as well as a central figure in Indian politics both before and after India's Independence. He was the prime minister from India's Independence 1947 till his death in 1964. He was also known as Pandit Nehru and Chacha Nehru, and his birth anniversary is marked as Children's Day in India.

7. Linguistic

Chennai:

The Tamil name of the erstwhile Madras.

Kozhikode:

The Malayalam name of Calicut.

Malayali:

A person from the Indian state of Kerala.

Keralites:

Malayalis are also referred to as Keralites.

Mumbai:

The Marathi name of the erstwhile Bombay.

8. Political

Gulf Cooperation Council Countries:

The Gulf Cooperation Council (GCC) is a political and economic union of Arab states in the Arabian Gulf. It was established in 1981 and its six members are the United Arab Emirates, Saudi Arabia, Qatar, Oman, Kuwait and Bahrain.

Niyamasabha:

It is the Malayalam term for the Kerala Legislative Assembly.

Acknowledgements

THE INSPIRATION THAT AMMA and Achan—the late Susheela and Madhava Menon—provided by the lives they lived, moulded me. They gave me unfettered freedom to be who I was and what I wanted to be, without any undue coercion and pressures, while at the same time, drawing *Lakshman Rekhas* (boundaries that are meant to protect) that prescribed limits that I knew I should not transcend while treading through life.

My three siblings—Indira Chechi, Unnikrishnan Chettan, Sathi Devi—with their unconditional love and bonding ensured that very early on in life and while growing up, whenever I had a weak, trying moment, a familial safety net would always provide the required salve and help me negotiate those little bumps on the road so that I could get back on track.

Now, on the perch that I have reached after a long and winding climb with Girija, I am eternally thankful to the gods above for helping us weave together an eyrie, a warm and cosy nest with Aravind, Madhav and Govind, the warmth of whose hearth keeps my fire burning, inspiring me to go further and ignite the passions of entrepreneurship, empathy and humanity in our kids and even among the youth of Kerala, India and the world in whatever capacity I can.

This book is such an offering.

—∞—

The seed of this book was first sown in my mind by Sudhir Kumar, Senior Partner and Corporate Communications Head at Kreston Menon.

Our relationship goes back a long way, much before he joined us in 2006.

Broaching the idea of the book in early 2017, he said that my interesting life and the winding path I had walked from the rustic villages of Kerala to Dubai, and the eventful transformation of my career and professional life as an entrepreneur, would make for a compelling read.

Initially, I was not keen, believing that I was too young to be writing a book about myself, and I shelved the idea.

But Sudhir was very convinced and persistent.

As months passed, the constant messaging, reinforcement through subliminal and overt communication, and the use of the agenda-setting function—all classical communications playbook moves working in tandem—found their mark.

I was beginning to consider it.

The clincher was when Sudhir made me aware of the possibility that the book could inspire students and young entrepreneurs.

Whether that happens or not, the thought convinced me to give it a try.

My sincere thanks to Sudhir for pushing me into writing this book. Without his persuasion, this would never have happened.

To the extended Kreston Menon family of over 500 people in the Gulf Cooperation Council Countries and India, with whom I spend most of my waking hours, a big, heartfelt thanks for helping me grow into what I am today.

From atop my perch, I bow in sincere gratitude to all.

About the Author

RAJU MENON MCom, LLB, FCA, CPA, FAIA
Chairman and Managing Partner
Kreston Menon Group, UAE

IT WAS 28 YEARS ago that Raju Menon started 'Kreston Menon' as a three-member practice, which at present is one of the leading Auditing and Consulting firms in UAE.

The Founder, Chairman and Managing Partner of Kreston Menon, Raju is a fellow member of the Institute of Chartered Accountants of India, fellow member of Association of International Accountants (FAIA), UK, and qualified the CPA Examination of USA.

Raju Menon served as the Chairman of the Dubai Chapter of the Institute of Chartered Accountants of India during the year 2014–15, which is the largest overseas chapter with more than 3,000 members.

Raju was listed in the coveted 'Forbes Top 100 Leaders in the Arab World' for 6 consecutive years and has won many prestigious awards for his contributions to the profession, economy and society.

Kreston Menon was awarded the 'Superbrand' status for the 9th successive year by the Superbrands Council of UAE, which bears testimony to the leadership excellence of Raju Menon. Being extremely mindful of an organization's responsibility to society, he has ensured that the group is passionately involved in wide-ranging CSR activities as well as Diversity & Inclusion initiatives.

Kreston Menon offers a wide range of services including Audit and Assurance, Taxation Services, Business and Technology Consulting through its 500 professionals in 11 verticals across 17 offices in the Gulf countries and India.

Kreston Menon is a member of Kreston Global, the 13th largest global network of independent accounting firms, headquartered in London, which has 200 firms in 110 countries and is home to more than 23,000 dedicated professionals.